Syllable Structure and
Stress in Spanish

Linguistic Inquiry Monographs
Samuel Jay Keyser, general editor

Syllable Structure and
Stress in Spanish

A Nonlinear Analysis

James W. Harris

The MIT Press
Cambridge, Massachusetts
London, England

This book was set in VIP Times Roman by Village Typographers, Inc., and
printed and bound by Halliday Lithograph in the United States of America.

Library of Congress Cataloging in Publication Data

Harris, James W. (James Wesley)
  Syllable structure and stress in Spanish.

  (Linguistic inquiry monographs ; 8)
  Bibliography: p.
  Includes index.
  1. Spanish language—Syllabication.   2. Spanish language—Prosodic
analysis. I. Title. II. Series.
PC4168.H37 1983   461'.6   82–18638
ISBN 0–262–08124–5 (hard)
ISBN 0–262–58060–8 (pbk.)

5-5-88
at

Contents

Contents

Series Foreword

We are pleased to present this monograph as the eighth in the series *Linguistic Inquiry Monographs*. These monographs will present new and original research beyond the scope of the article, and we hope they will benefit our field by bringing to it perspectives that will stimulate further research and insight.

Originally published in limited edition, the *Linguistic Inquiry Monograph* series is now available on a much wider scale. This change is due to the great interest engendered by the series and the needs of a growing readership. The editors wish to thank the readers for their support and welcome suggestions about future directions the series might take.

Samuel Jay Keyser
for the Editorial Board

Acknowledgments

I would like to express my gratitude to the following people for help they gave me, in one way or another, in the preparation of this study: Pilar Beléndez, Ivonne Bordelois, Heles Contreras, Francesco D'Introno, Manuel Elías, Paloma García-Bellido, John Goldsmith, Mauricio González, Jorge Guitart, Morris Halle, Bruce Hayes, Paul Kiparsky, Carmen Lozano, Gonzalo Mascareñas, Joan Mascaró, Yves-Charles Morin, Carlos Otero, Graciela Rosemberg, Elisabeth Selkirk, Donca Steriade, Margarita Suñer, and anonymous reviewers for The MIT Press. I also profited from interaction with professors and students, too numerous to mention by name, at the Universidad Nacional Autónoma de México and El Colegio de México, where I lectured on some of this material in the spring of 1981.

SYLLABLE STRUCTURE
IN SPANISH

Introduction to Part I

The prosodic properties of language are currently under intense study. There is a feeling in the air that a significant page has been turned in the study of phonology and that we may be witnessing or about to witness a genuine breakthrough.[1] Even so, the general theory of syllabic organization is still quite rudimentary, and current studies of the syllable structure of particular languages represent a variety of approaches and ideas. Although it is hardly necessary to emphasize that the present monograph is neither exhaustive nor definitive, I do feel that it has reached a stage of development at which interesting questions have been dealt with clearly enough to warrant its being made available in its present form to interested investigators. Chapter 1 lays the empirical groundwork for a theory of syllable structure in Spanish, chapter 2 presents a fairly explicit account of language-particular rules and universal principles that underlie the primary data, and chapter 3 shows how the theory thus developed can illuminate several classical problems in Spanish phonology and a few problems that have come to light only recently.

The two most fully articulated studies of Spanish syllable structure that I know are those of Saporta and Contreras (1962) and Hooper (1976, chapters 10–12). In the former the organization of words into syllables is specified basically by a phrase structure grammar which generates hierarchical structures of terminal and nonterminal elements. On Hooper's account, on the other hand, syllables are organized linearly rather than hierarchically; the descriptive device is a template consisting of a string of positions (bounded at each end by the symbol $) with which are associated conditions of "consonantal strength." The material presented here will demonstrate that both of these pioneering works are observationally and descriptively inadequate. Furthermore, it will lead to the conclusion that neither a phrase structure component nor a linear template is among the formal mechanisms that play a role in the specification of syllable structure. Rather, intrasyllabic organization is to be ascribed to (a) a set of rules that apply to strings of phonemes supplied by the lexicon, collecting groups of segments into a labeled constituent, and (b) a set of filters that mark constituents as deviant under specified conditions.

Why study syllable structure? The most elementary response is the mountain climber's answer: because it's there. Without question, dealing with syllables in some way or other is part of speakers' competence in their native language.[2] Syllables thus constitute a legitimate object of linguistic investigation in their own right.

Syllable structure also interacts with other aspects of linguistic organization. This can perhaps be most immediately appreciated by considering the contribution of the syllable to phonotactics, that is, generalizations concerning the sequential distribution of phonemes. It can easily be established that the unit of linguistic organization over which phonotactic constraints hold is primarily the syllable, not, say, the morpheme or the word. Whatever else they may be, words are at least strings of syllables. Thus, the definition of "possible word" in some language can be derived in large part from the definition of "possible syllable" in that language. We must not oversimplify, however. Words are not just strings of syllables, and the phonological organization of words is not exhausted by statements of syllable-level constraints. In particular, such constraints do not replace phonological rules, of which some are sensitive to syllable structure and some are not.

Phonological rules are not the only type of generalizations that interact with syllable structure. Spanish provides an example in which a morphological generalization depends on syllable structure in an interesting way. In certain classes of words in many dialects, the selection of the allomorph of the diminutive suffix depends on the number of syllables in the base word. (For detailed discussion, see Jaeggli (1980).) For example, the diminutive of disyllabic *madre* is *madrecita* (**madrita*), while that of trisyllabic *comadre* is *comadrita* (**comadrecita*). Now consider the pair *espacio* and *despacio*. Their diminutives are *espaciecito* (**espacito*) and *despacito* (**despaciecito*). Why should they be different? More strangely, why does trisyllabic *es-pa-cio* take the same allomorph *-ecitV* as disyllabic words like *madre?* We can answer these questions if we count the syllables of *espacio* in exactly the right way. (*Des-pa-ci-to,* like *co-ma-dri-ta,* poses no problem.) We must disregard the initial *e,* which, as is well known, is epenthetic; and we must know that the last two segments *i* and *o* are not both syllabic. Thus, the structure that selects the allomorph *-ecitV* is disyllabic *spa-cio.* In other words, the relevant morphological rule requires as input a representation in which syllable structure assignment has been started but not completed: the segments represented by orthographic *i* and *o* must have been gathered into some inclusive unit, but initial *e* must remain unincorporated.

Constituent organization versus boundary markers. The environment / ___ {C,#} is seen often in phonological descriptions—I will cite several instances in the course of this monograph, especially in chapter 3. It has been argued that this disjunction is simply a cryptic way of saying "syllable boundary"; thus, to the extent that the descriptions in question are empirically justified, syllable boundaries should be granted recognition in linguistic theory.[3]

I will support a stronger claim here. The Spanish data to be examined reveal a number of generalizations which require reference to intrasyllabic organization rather than intersyllabic boundaries. Direct reference to boundaries in these cases would in fact result in a loss of generalization. Now, when intrasyllabic organization is adequately represented, the location and nature of syllable boundaries are automatically provided. Therefore, special symbols (such as "$") that serve only to mark the position of syllable boundaries in strings of segments are otiose. Occam's razor demands that phonological theory exclude them. Of course, we may still use "$" or "–", or any other symbol, as handy typographical expedients, so long as we clearly recognize their (lack of) theoretical status.[4]

Every linguistic description that contains either an explicit boundary symbol or the cryptic notation / ___ {C,#} thus constitutes a challenge: either it must be reformulable with equal or greater descriptive adequacy in terms of internal syllabic organization, or the more restrictive (and hence a priori more desirable) theory that eschews the allegedly functionless machinery must be abandoned. I will present an analysis that meets that challenge with respect to cases in the recent literature of Spanish in which the alternative is argued clearly.

Chapter 1
Basic Data

1.1 Constituent Structure

Consider the word *buey* 'ox'. This much is clear and uncontroversial: *buey* consists of a single syllable. Other matters, however, are not so cut-and-dried. Does *buey* have any internal phonological organization beyond the level of the segment? If so, what is it? Is it correctly represented, for example, by one of the following hierarchical structures?[1]

(1.1)

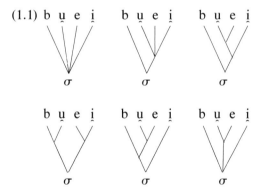

Discussion of such questions in the literature of Spanish is rare. The most lucid treatment that I know is that of Saporta and Contreras (1962). They propose that the Spanish syllable has a ternary-branching organization whose primary constituents are the *onset* (O), the *nucleus* (N), and the *coda* (C), of which the first and last are optional:

(1.2) (Onset)   Nucleus   (Coda)

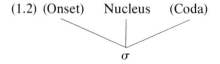

Saporta and Contreras's grammar assigns to *buey* the structure shown in (1.3), which has a nonbranching onset, a ternary-branching nucleus, and an empty coda:

(1.3)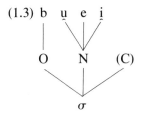

The coda position is filled by the final consonantal segment in words like *buen, bien, pues:*

(1.4)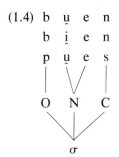

   The authors of the 1973 *Esbozo de una nueva gramática,* sponsored by the Real Academia Española, propose exactly the same structures suggested by Saporta and Contreras. However, there is a striking difference between the two treatments. The *Esbozo* simply asserts without argument that Spanish syllables have a given structure. Saporta and Contreras, on the other hand, state explicitly their motivation for constructing a grammar that generates the representations it does rather than other logically possible and a priori plausible structures. Their primary criterion is "economy," or "simplicity," for which they painstakingly develop a precise definition.[2]
   In the following discussion, I will justify a rather different view of the structure of *buey* in particular and Spanish syllables in general, as suggested in (1.5):

(1.5) a. (Onset)   Rhyme   b. b u e i

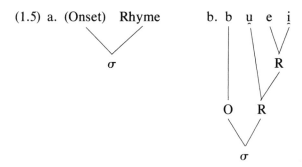

As (1.5a) shows, the syllable has two immediate constituents—not three—namely, the *onset* (O) and the *rhyme* (R). The rhyme is the obligatory constituent containing the sonority peak (always a vowel in Spanish, not necessarily so in other languages), and the onset is its optional left sister. As we shall see, evidence for the existence of a rhyme constituent, in the technical sense of *constituent,* is overwhelming. (The same is true in other languages; see the references in note 1 of the introduction.) As (1.5b) suggests, the rhyme constituent has its own internal structure, but, as we shall see, the evidence countermotivates recognizing a theoretically significant "coda" constituent. More specifically, structures like the one shown in (1.5b) are the least complex ones that can support the generalizations that we will discover. To single out some unit and label it "coda" would in fact result in loss of generality both in the principles of rhyme structure and in the interaction of these structures with other phonological phenomena.

Halle and Vergnaud (1980, 93) provides the following interesting comment:

Our studies have uncovered many phonological processes where the constituents of the syllable—in particular, the onset and rimes—function independently of one another. In fact, it appears to us that the superordinate unit, the syllable, plays a much more marginal role in phonology than do its constituents.

Evidence of this sort of "independence" makes a convincing case for constituency. Spanish onsets and rhymes are largely independent in the way suggested; in particular, as we shall see, the two categories have distinct principles of internal organization. Before examining this matter, however, I will sketch two arguments that support the division of Spanish syllables into two major constituents, without taking into account the details of their internal organization.

First Argument. Spanish syllables contain at most five segments.[3]
For example, the first syllable of the following words is of the maximum length permitted:

(1.6) 1 2 3 4 5

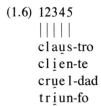

claus-tro
clien-te
cruel-dad
triun-fo

Consider, however, the following cases:

(1.7) a. *Disallowed:*   1 2 3 4 5

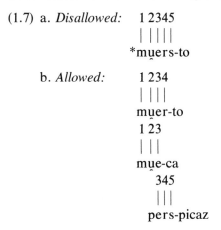

*muers-to

   b. *Allowed:*   1 2 3 4

muer-to

1 2 3

mue-ca

3 4 5

pers-picaz

These examples illustrate the fact that not all five-segment syllables are
allowed (1.7a), although identical substrings of up to three and four
segments are permissible (1.7b). If the overall length of the first syllable
of (1.7a) is not excessive and none of its subsequences is ruled out, to
what can its ill-formedness be ascribed? Assigning an internal structure
to the initial syllables of (1.6) and (1.7) provides an answer:

(1.8) a. cl aus-tro   cl ien-te   cr uel-dad   tr iun-fo

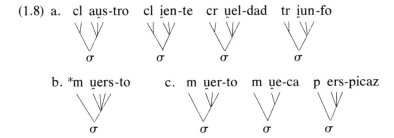

   b. *m uers-to   c. m uer-to   m ue-ca   p ers-picaz

The leftmost constituent contains the initial string of consonantal segments and the other one contains the remaining segments in the syllable. For convenience we can call these constituents the *onset* and the
rhyme, respectively, although in the present context nothing hinges on
the labeling. Given the structures of (1.8), the empirically correct generalization can be stated: the rhyme can contain at most three segments. If these constituent groupings are not recognized, a statement
like this becomes necessary: Spanish syllables have a maximum length
of five segments if the initial string of consonants contains two segments, but a maximum length of four segments if there is one initial
consonant, and three segments if there is no initial consonant. One has
only to formulate this (non)alternative to see its inadequacy: in fact,
rhymes are maximally three segments long independently of onset
length.

The grammar of Saporta and Contreras (1962) classifies syllables like
muers- in (1.7a) as well formed, assigning them the following structure:

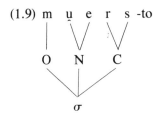

Each of the three constituents O(nset), N(ucleus), and C(oda) contains
permissible sequences; some additional stipulation is required to de-
clare the entire syllable ill formed. As we have just seen, the empirically correct form of this stipulation involves reference to a constituent
that subsumes the nucleus and the coda of (1.9).[4]

Second Argument. As is well known, antepenultimate stress is possible in nonverb forms in Spanish if the penult is open, but not if the
penult is checked by a consonant:

(1.10) telé-fo-no   *vs.*   *telé-fos-no
                            *telé-fol-po

Words like *teléfosno, *teléfolpo* are not simply accidentally missing;
they are judged to be ill formed by native speakers.

Antepenultimate stress is also impossible if the penult is closed by a
glide:

(1.11) *telé-boi-na
        *telé-cau-sa

Words like those in (1.11) are also systematically ruled out rather than simply nonexistent. There is, of course, nothing wrong with such forms as purely segmental strings, as is shown by actual words like *boina, causa* and hypothetical words like *telebóina, telecáusa,* all of which are well formed.

More interestingly but less well known, antepenultimate stress is impossible in Spanish nonverb forms also if the vowel of the penult is preceded by a glide:

(1.12) *telé-fio-no
        *telé-fie-no
        *telé-fia-no
        *telé-fue-no
        *telé-fua-no

Again, all of these are impeccable as purely segmental strings and all are judged to be not accidentally missing but instead systematically excluded as nouns and adjectives.[5]

To what can the impossibility of antepenultimate stress in these three cases be attributed? We might guess that it somehow involves the length of the penultimate syllable. Notice, however, the following cases, in which antepenultimate stress is perfectly acceptable:

(1.13)   telé-gra-fo
         polí-glo-ta
         demó-cra-ta
         repú-bli-ca
         pú-tri-do
         Á-fri-ca

Such words show that the overall length of the penult is irrelevant, since three-segment penults are compatible with antepenultimate stress in (1.13) but not in (1.10)–(1.12). We seem to be left with statements like "antepenultimate stress is impossible if within the penult the vowel is preceded or followed by a glide, or followed by a consonant," or "antepenultimate stress is incompatible with a three-segment penult unless the first two segments of the penult are both consonants." Clearly, however, such complex statements reduce to a simple generalization if we recognize syllable-internal constituents as shown in (1.14):

(1.14) a. telé-gr a-fo   Á-fr i-ca

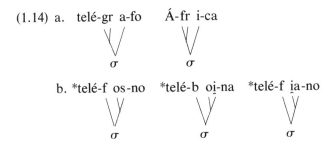

b. *telé-f os-no *telé-b oi̯-na *telé-f i̯a-no

As in (1.8), the first intrasyllabic constituent contains the initial string of consonantal segments and the second contains the remaining segments. The generalization that emerges is that antepenultimate stress is impossible if the second constituent contains more than one segment (the first constituent being irrelevant); or, in more familiar terminology,

(1.15) Antepenultimate stress is impossible if the penult contains a branching rhyme.

Now consider this material in the light of the grammar of Saporta and Contreras (1962), which assigns structure to the relevant cases as follows:

(1.16) a. Á-fr i -ca

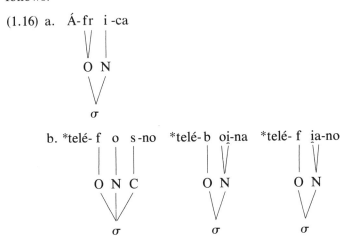

b. *telé- f o s -no   *telé-b oi̯-na   *telé- f i̯a-no

The best generalization that can be made in terms of the structures in (1.16) is the following:

(1.17) Antepenultimate stress is impossible if the penult contains
either a nonnull coda *or* a branching nucleus.

Comparison of (1.15) and (1.17) demonstrates clearly that failure to
recognize a constituent that embraces both nucleus and coda, namely
the rhyme, directly entails the loss of a significant generalization. (I will
place generalization (1.15) in a broader empirical and theoretical context in chapter 2.)

In this section, I have given an initial argument for two intrasyllabic
constituents above the level of the segment, which I will call *onset* and
rhyme. This argument takes the standard form for constituency arguments, namely, that postulating the constituents in question makes possible the statement of generalizations that would otherwise be lost. I
turn now to an examination of the internal structure of Spanish onsets
and rhymes. Of primary interest is the rhyme constituent, whose organization poses especially intriguing questions. For the sake of perspective, however, I will first briefly outline the structure of onsets.

1.2 Onsets

The onset is an optional constituent of the syllable in Spanish. Syllables
without onsets occur freely in all positions, e.g., *o-í-a, e-bre-o, is-la,
ca-ra-o-ta,* etc.

Onsets may consist of one or two segments. Any consonantal segment of the language may constitute a one-segment onset.[6] An illustrative sample appears in (1.18), which is arrayed in the same way as the
display of consonantal segments in note 6.

(1.18) za-pato	pa-to	o-cho	sa-co
a-bajo	de-do	(ma-ya)	ha-go
en-fermo	ca-sa	(ma-ya)	ca-ja
ca-ma	ca-na	ca-ña	
	ma-la	(ma-lla)	
	ca-ro		

I have illustrated these onsets in word-internal position since not all of
them occur freely in word-initial position.[7]

Two-segment onsets consist of a single obstruent followed by one of
the liquids *l* or *r*. (1.19) contains a sample of the occurring clusters:

(1.19) preso   com-pro   tres   o-tro   (*čr)   crema   mi-crobio
       plano   co-pla   (tlaco) (a-tleta) (*čl)   claro   an-cla
       brazo   a-bre   drama   a-drede   gris   a-grio
       blando ha-blo   (*dl)   globo   i-glesia
       frío   A-frica   (*sr)   (Jruschef)
       flan   a-flicto (*sl)

The same two-segment onsets are permitted in word-initial and word-internal position.[8] As shown, all of the labials *p, b, f* and the velars *k* and *g* cluster freely with both *l* and *r*. Among the dentals, *t* clusters freely with *r* in all dialects and marginally with *l* (see note 8), *d* clusters only with *r*, and *s* does not cluster at all. Palatal *č* and velar *x* occur only in one-segment onsets (but see note 8 regarding [xr]). I will return to this oddly skewed distribution in section 2.4. Meanwhile, I will summarize this section by stating informally the following rules:

(1.20) *Rule O1:* Any consonantal segment may constitute an onset.

      Rule O2: An obstruent followed by a liquid may constitute an onset.

1.3 Rhymes

Example (1.21) displays a survey of Spanish rhyme types:

(1.21)

		Medial	*Final*			*Medial*	*Final*
a.	1. *V*	pa-ta	tapa	b.	1. *Vs*	pas-ta	res
	2. *VG*	au-tor	lei		2. *VGs*	claus-tro	seis
	3. *VL*	sal-ta	mar		3. *VLs*	pers-picaz	vals
	4. *VN*	com-pra	sartén		4. *VNs*	mons-truo	Mayans
	5. *VO*	seg-mento	red		5. *VOs*	abs-tracto	Félix [feliks]
	6. *VGL*	*	*		6. *VGLs*	*	*
	7. *VGN*	(*)	*		7. *VGNs*	*	*
	8. *VGO*	(*)	*		8. *VGOs*	*	*
c.	1. *GV*	nue-vo	apio	d.	1. *GVs*	fies-ta	pues
	2. *GVG*	(*)	buei		2. *GVGs*	*	(*)
	3. *GVL*	fuer-te	fiel		3. *GVLs*	*	*
	4. *GVN*	siem-pre	Juan		4. *GVNs*	*	*
	5. *GVO*	diag-nosis	Goliat		5. *GVOs*	*	*

6. *GVGL* *	*	6. *GVGLs* *	*
7. *GVGN* *	*	7. *GVGNs* *	*
8. *GVGO* *	*	8. *GVGOs* *	*

The quadrants of (1.21) are organized according to the following system:

(i) Within each quadrant, the order of rhymes follows the familiar sonority scale V > G > L > N > O.

(ii) The two upper quadrants have rhymes beginning with V; the two lower quadrants have the same rhymes preceded by G.

(iii) The two right quadrants have rhymes corresponding to those in the left quadrants, plus *s*.

Below are some general observations about this material. Parenthesized asterisks indicate rhyme types about which native judgments require interpretation and other special cases to which I will return after surveying the basic facts.

(a) Spanish does not have syllabic consonants; every Spanish rhyme contains a vowel.[9]

(b) All rhyme types in (1.21) with one or two segments are well formed, as are most rhymes with three segments. Longer rhymes are ill formed.

(c) For every permissible V-initial rhyme type in (1.21a,b) there is a corresponding permissible G-initial type in (1.21c,d), up to the maximum length of three segments.

(d) The phoneme /s/ has a special status not shared with any other segments: for every permissible rhyme type in (1.21a,c) not ending in /s/ there is a corresponding permissible *s*-final type in (1.21b,d), up to the maximum length of three segments.

(e) Rhyme types other than those shown in (1.21) are impossible in Spanish. For example, *VLN, *VLO, *VNO (for O ≠ /s/) are ill formed even though they neither exceed the three-segment maximum length nor violate the sonority scale V > G > L > N > O. No rhyme type of any length is allowed that violates this scale.[10]

The special cases flagged by parenthesized asterisks are these:

(f) VGN rhymes (1.21a7) apparently do not occur at all word-finally, and are found in only three words in word-medial position: *vein-te, trein-ta, aun-que*. Native speakers vigorously reject nonce words with these rhymes, and then become confused when confronted with one of the above examples. My interpretation of these reactions is that VGN rhymes are ungrammatical and that the three words just mentioned are lexicalized deviant forms, like English *svelte, vroom,* etc.

(g) VGO rhymes (1.21a8)—for O ≠ /s/—are even more marginal than VGN. I can find only one instance, that of the stem of *auxilio* [au̯k-sili̯o]. Native reactions in this case are the same as for VGN. I thus draw the same conclusion, namely, that VGO rhymes (O ≠ /s/) are ungrammatical in all positions and that the stem of *auxilio* is an extra-systematic oddity.

(h) GVG rhymes (1.21c2) occur in final position in a small number of words in general use like *bu̯ei̯, Paragu̯ai̯, Bi̯oi̯* and in internal position in a few words of limited currency, mostly proper names like *Cu̯au̯-tla, Cuauhtemoc* [ku̯au̯-témok], *Guale-gu̯ai̯-chu,* whose indigenous origin is strongly felt. Native speakers tend to make weak and vacillating judgments about the well-formedness of GVG rhymes. Thus, their characterization in (1.21) as permissible word-finally but impermissible internally is rather arbitrary.

(i) GVGs rhymes (1.21d2) are unquestionably impossible in word-internal position. In word-final position they occur only in the special case mentioned in note 3, namely, second person plural verb forms, which are not used in Latin American dialects. There is thus no reason to consider them as part of our data. I will, however, make one further remark later about the fact that the final -Gs in these verb forms is an inflectional ending, unlike any other element illustrated in (1.21).

1.4 Rhyme-Internal Cooccurrence Restrictions

1.4.1 Liquids
As (1.21) illustrates, liquids occur within rhymes only after vowels and before *s*. Both *r* and *l* occur after all five vowels:

(1.22) car-ta   ter-co   cor-to   mir-to   tur-co
       sal-ta   sel-va   col-mo   mil-pa   mul-ta

Both *r* and *l* occur before *s: pers-pectiva, sols-ticio.* In short, there are no cooccurrence restrictions involving liquids and other segments within rhymes.

1.4.2 Nasals
From (1.21) we also see that nasals occur within rhymes only after vowels and before *s*. Nasals occur freely after all five vowels:

(1.23) sam-ba   hem-bra   som-bra   mim-bre   zum-ba
       man-ta   men-te   mon-to   pin-to   pun-to

The only nasal that can precede s, however, is n:

(1.24)
$$
mo \left\{ \begin{array}{l} \text{ns-} \\ \text{*ms-} \\ \text{*ñs-} \\ \text{*ŋs-} \end{array} \right\} truo
$$

This is not an exclusively rhyme-internal restriction but rather a consequence of a general word-level constraint that nasals agree in point of
articulation with a following obstruent. In short, there are no cooccurrence restrictions particular to rhymes involving nasals and other
segments.

1.4.3 Glides
Inspection of (1.21) reveals that glides occur before s, before nasals,
and adjacent to vowels, on either side. Most GV and VG sequences are
well formed:

(1.25) Vi̯:   hai̯   pei̯-ne   *   oi̯-go   mui̯
       i̯V: di̯a-blo bi̯en   *   pi̯o-jo   vi̯u-da
       Vu̯:   au̯-to   Eu̯-ropa ci̯u-dad bou̯   *
       u̯V: cu̯al   cu̯e-va   cu̯i-da   cu̯o-ta   *

The exclusions are systematic: glides cannot occur adjacent to a high
vowel that agrees in roundness (which always coincides with frontness
in nonlow vowels in Spanish):

(1.26) *i̯i *ii̯ *u̯u *uu̯

Cooccurrence restrictions involving glides and vowels are thus dramat-
ically different from those involving other pairs of segment types: the
sequences in (1.26) are utterly unpronounceable in Spanish rhymes.[11] I
will return to these data in section 2.4.

1.4.4 Obstruents
Obstruents other than s are relatively infrequent in Spanish rhymes. A
tally of the rhymes on several pages of current Mexico City newspapers
reveals that sonorant consonants outnumber obstruents other than s by
a ratio of approximately seven to one in this context. More specifically,
an average page has a little over 600 rhymes with sonorant consonants

versus fewer than 100 rhymes with obstruents other than *s*.[12] The significance of these figures is unclear. On the one hand, the seven-to-one preponderance of sonorants over obstruents suggests a difference in status, perhaps a distinction in markedness. On the other hand, the fact that approximately 85 examples of such unremarkable words as *pac-to*, *ap-to*, *ob-jeto*, *indig-no*, *elec-ci*ón can be found on a single page of a general newspaper dictates that rhymes containing obstruents other than *s* cannot be regarded as bizarre or somehow illegitimate. Perhaps an analogy would be helpful. It is known that /u/ is the least frequent of the five Spanish vowels, by a considerable margin (Navarro Tomás (1965, 74–75)). But no one would take this fact as evidence that Spanish words with /u/ are ill formed. Why should the same not be true of rhymes with obstruents? Until some argument is advanced to the contrary, I see no reason not to consider the rhymes in question as fully well formed.[13]

Chapter 2
Principles of Organization

2.1 Language-Particular Rules and Universal Conditions

To examine how the class of syllable structures in Spanish is specified, I begin with the premise that not every fact about Spanish syllable structure is a fact about Spanish. Put less paradoxically, certain aspects of Spanish syllable structure are instantiations of universal properties, to be attributed to the general theory of syllables rather than to the grammar of Spanish. For example, the fact that Spanish onsets, rhymes, and whole syllables have (maximally) binary branching is presumably a universal property of prosodic structure.[1] On the other hand, it seems to be a peculiarity of Spanish that rhymes contain at most three segments. Thus, a statement to this effect, but not one about binarity, rings up a cost in the grammar of Spanish. In short, the operation of language-particular syllable structure rules is under the surveillance of universal well-formedness conditions. I will interpret Kiparsky's (1979) proposals for universally unmarked syllable structure, with which I assume familiarity, as a set of such conditions. On this interpretation, Spanish syllable structure rules are constrained to produce an output with maximally binary-branching trees meeting the maximality and simplicity requirements, matching the universal sonority scale, and so on. Departures from these conditions are either costly or prohibited outright.

I know of only one fully explicit proposal concerning the specification of syllable structure in Spanish, namely, Saporta and Contreras (1962). There the analogy with syntax (i.e., the syntax of the period) is virtually perfect: a context-sensitive phrase structure grammar generates both terminal elements (phonemes) and nonterminal elements (the node labels S(yllable), O(nset), N(ucleus), and C(oda); a transformational component performs certain deletions and other mop-up operations.

I view the specification of syllable structure rather differently. Following Fudge (1969) and others, I ascribe intrasyllabic organization to two distinct types of principles. In Fudge's terminology, these are *colligational* and *collocational restrictions*. Colligational restrictions determine the geometric arrangements of major classes of segments, while collocational restrictions state cooccurrence constraints on individual members of these classes. In the terms used here, the former set of principles comprises a component of *rules* that assign a labeled hierarchical structure to a string of phonemes supplied by the lexicon; the latter set are contained in a component of *filters* that mark certain constituents as deviant.

I turn now to the first component, beginning with the structure of onsets.

2.2 The Onset Rule

Two informal rules for the formation of syllable onsets in Spanish are given in (1.20) as a summary of section 1.2. The following is a more general (hence, more desirable) statement:

(2.1) *Generalized Onset Rule (Preliminary Version)*
    Construct a maximally binary-branching tree of category
    O(nset) whose branches dominate [+consonantal] segments.

This rule characterizes the two structures shown in (2.2) with representative examples:[2]

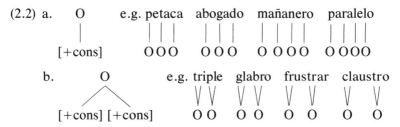

(2.2) a.   O   e.g. petaca   abogado   mañanero   paralelo

    [+cons]   O O O   O O O   O O O O   O O O O

    b.   O   e.g. triple   glabro   frustrar   claustro

    [+cons] [+cons]   O O   O O   O O   O O

The nonbranching structure shown in (2.2a) is not problematic in any way, since any consonant can be a one-segment onset. In the case of the branching structure (2.2b), however, rule (2.1) overgenerates, as illustrated in (2.3):

(2.3)

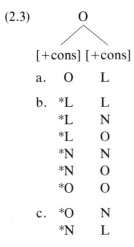

[+cons] [+cons]

a. O   L

b. *L   L
    *L   N
    *L   O
    *N   N
    *N   O
    *O   O

c. *O   N
    *N   L

Only obstruent-plus-liquid clusters (2.3a) constitute well-formed two-segment onsets in Spanish. How then are the clusters in (2.3b) and (2.3c) to be ruled out? The universal sonority scale establishes that in the unmarked case the left-to-right order of [+consonantal] segments in onsets is obstruent–nasal–liquid. Thus, the unacceptable clusters in (2.3b), which do not match this order, are excluded by the general theory, that is, by simply introducing no complication in rule (2.1) or elsewhere in the grammar of Spanish.

The unacceptable clusters *ON and *NL of (2.3c), on the other hand, do not violate the universal sonority scale and thus must be excluded by some language-particular stipulation. Notice that unacceptable *ON and *NL contain segments that are adjacent on the scale obstruent–nasal–liquid, unlike well-formed OL. This observation allows us to make maximal use of universal grammar to effect the necessary language-particular restriction, namely, by requiring that two-segment onsets contain consonants that are not adjacent on the sonority scale. The revised rule reads as follows:

(2.4) *Onset Rule (Final Version)*
      Construct a maximally binary branching tree of category
      O(nset) whose branches dominate [+consonantal] segments
      that are not adjacent on the universal sonority scale.

Rule (2.4) is superior to (2.1) in that (2.4) is appropriately constrained so as not to generate unwanted onset types. Rule (2.4) is superior to the original set of rules (1.20) in that (2.4) does not duplicate the work of the universal sonority scale in specifying the order of segments in branching onsets. I suspect that it could also be argued that the "non-adjacency" stipulation of (2.4) represents the universally unmarked case: surely obstruent–liquid clusters are more natural onsets than obstruent–nasal and nasal–liquid clusters.

In sum, once we take the contribution of the universal theory of syllables into account, it becomes evident that the Spanish Onset Rule (2.4) is highly, perhaps maximally, unmarked. First, as noted above, the binary branching of prosodic structure can be attributed to the general theory. Second, onsets comprised of [+consonantal] segments presumably represent the universally unmarked case. Third, although it is peculiar to Spanish that onsets cannot exceed two segments in length, longer onsets are presumably more marked than shorter ones. I conclude that rule (2.4) is about as close to "cost free" in the grammar of Spanish as it could be.

What remains to be accounted for on a language-particular, even dialect-particular, basis are the cooccurrence restrictions among onset segments—for example, the fact that *tr* and *dr* are permissible in all dialects, *tl* is permissible in some dialects but not in others, and *dl* is ruled out in all dialects. I will take up these restrictions in section 2.4.

2.3 Rhyme Rules

2.3.1 Spanish Rhyme Structure
Spanish rhymes are obviously more complex than onsets. This gross observation is reflected in the fact that the grammar contains only one highly unmarked onset rule but several rhyme rules of varying degrees of complexity.

Given that Spanish rhymes consist of one, two, or three segments, exactly four configurations of binary tree structures are possible:

(2.5) a. one segment:

b. two segments:

c. three segments:

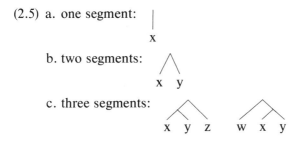

I will argue that all four of these configurations occur. More specifically, the geometric structure of Spanish rhymes conforms to the following two "templates":

(2.6) a. 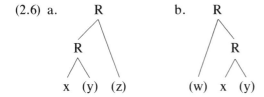 b.

As shown, Spanish rhymes are left- or right-branching structures with at most one embedding. The templates themselves are not the fundamental organizing principles of rhymes, but rather (somewhat imprecise) representations of the output of a more highly articulated set of principles. These principles can be stated roughly as follows:

(2.7) a. A basic Rhyme Rule R1 characterizes "core" structures of
the form R

[+syllabic] ([−syllabic])

   b. The core may acquire a periphery by *one* of the following
      rules:
      (i) R2: A glide may be adjoined to the left of the core.
      (ii) R3: The phoneme /s/ may be adjoined to the right of the
           core.

These principles characterize all and only the basic rhyme configurations shown in (2.6). I will discuss these rules individually and in more detail in following subsections.

I have mentioned a number of times that Spanish rhymes are restricted to a maximum length of three segments. Templates (2.6a,b)— or rather the principles (2.7a,b) that generate the templates—in effect stipulate that Spanish rhymes have at most one embedding. This stipulation, together with the universal binarity of syllable structure trees, enforces the length restriction. A language-particular principle abetted by a general principle is better than pure stipulation, but it would obviously be preferable to derive the length restriction entirely from general principles, avoiding stipulation altogether. It is not clear to me at present that this is possible, however, so I leave the matter as a topic for future study.[3]

2.3.2 The Basic Rhyme Rule
The following rule constitutes the core of Spanish rhyme structure:

(2.8) *Rhyme Rule R1*
   Construct a maximally binary branching tree of category
   R(hyme) whose obligatory left branch dominates [+syllabic,
   −consonantal] and whose optional right branch dominates
   [−syllabic].

This rule characterizes the following structures (where the features
[syllabic] and [consonantal] are not node labels; see note 2):

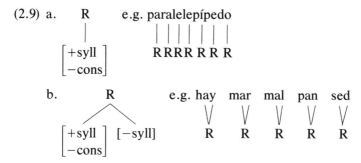

Like the Onset Rule (2.4), Rhyme Rule R1 ranks very low in markedness. The binary structure is of course attributable to the general theory. The fact that the syllabic segment must be [−consonantal] is not
charged against the grammar of Spanish, since vocalic syllable nuclei
are undoubtedly unmarked with respect to consonantal nuclei (i.e.,
syllabic consonants). Furthermore, the position of the nuclear vowel to
the left of the other segment is in accordance with Kiparsky's (1979)
condition that in branching rhymes the unmarked order of constituents
is (*s, w*) with respect to the sonority scale.
   If it is correct to assume that the feature [−consonantal] need not be
explicitly mentioned in R1, since this feature reflects the universally
unmarked case, then this rule requires access to no information other
than that contained in the *prosodic skeleton* of a word. The prosodic
skeleton is a highly improverished subrepresentation consisting only of
a string of the symbols C and V, which are understood to stand for
[−syllabic] and [+syllabic], respectively (plus of course [+segment]).[4]
Limiting access of syllable-tree-building rules to this impoverished subrepresentation greatly constrains the class of such rules, a highly desirable general result.

2.3.3 Rhyme Rule R2
As stated in (2.7), the basic rhyme structure generated by rule R1 can be further elaborated. The primary elaboration is governed by rule R2:

(2.10) *Rhyme Rule R2*
  Adjoin a [−consonantal] segment to a rhyme.

This rule adds the following to the inventory of rhyme structures in Spanish:[5]

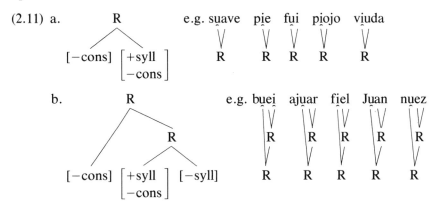

(2.11) a.

b.

The rhymes in (2.11a) result when the [−syllabic] option of R1 is not taken, and those in (2.11b) result when it is.

 We see in (2.11) the result of adjoining a [−consonantal] segment to the left side of an existing rhyme. Rule R2, however, does not specify to which side the new segment must attach. This seems not to be necessary. To see why, consider first the structure shown in (2.12):

(2.12)

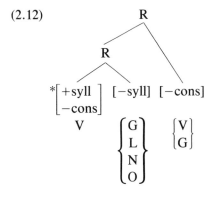

In this case, adjunction of a [−consonantal] segment on the right produces rhyme types that are universally prohibited because they violate the crescendo–decrescendo sonority pattern of syllable structure observed by Kiparsky and many others. This detail thus need not be specified as a part of the grammar of Spanish.

Now imagine the following derivation:

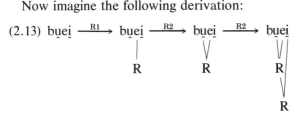

(2.13)

Here R2 has been allowed to apply first to the left and then to the right of an existing rhyme. This results in a left-branching structure instead of the right-branching structure shown for *buey* in (2.11b). This case, unlike that of (2.12), does not violate universal syllabic sonority requirements. Furthermore, I can detect no undesirable consequences associated with this structure for GVG rhymes within the phonology of Spanish. I assume, however, that the derivation shown in (2.13) is impossible in principle, because its first step violates a general convention requiring that prosodic-structure-building rules apply "maximally," that is, so as to incorporate all possible segments allowed by the rule (and other general conditions). Specifically, the initial application of R1 must result in (2.14):

(2.14) buei
        ⋁
        R

It seems fairly safe to guess, as we did in the case of R1, that the feature [−consonantal] in rule R2 represents the universally unmarked case. That is, it is presumably more natural for the first member of a rhyme to be a glide or a vowel than a consonant. If this is correct, then the cost of R2 in the grammar of Spanish is minimal, since everything about it except its presence in the grammar follows from the general theory.

2.3.4 The Special Behavior of /s/

We have repeatedly observed that /s/,[6] unlike any other segment, can attach to the right of any otherwise well-formed rhyme, so long as the three-segment length restriction is respected. Actually, /s/ appears to violate this restriction in one instance, which I will discuss (and dispense with) immediately. This is the case of verb forms like (2.15a,b), etc., which occur only in certain dialects (see note 3 of chapter 1 and observation (i) in the alphabetical list below (1.21)).

(2.15) a. limpiais   b. averigüeis

In such forms the last two segments -*is* constitute the second person plural inflectional morpheme, which is located outside the "derivational stem" (for example, *limpi* + *a-* = root plus theme vowel, and *averigu* + *e-* = root plus present subjunctive marker). I will argue in considerable detail in part II that consonants in this morphological environment are *extrametrical*. Extrametrical elements are regarded as simply "not there" or inaccessible to otherwise relevant rules. After the rules have passed them by, such elements are incorporated into prosodic structure by a general principle of *Stray Adjunction*. The language-particular stipulation that consonants outside the derivational stem are extrametrical, together with the universal stray-collecting principle, can explain the well-formedness of words like *limpiais, averigüeis* despite their apparent violation of the rhyme length restriction: the final /s/, being inflectional, is extrametrical and thus cannot be "seen" to be counted. Occurrences of /s/ inside stems are not extrametrical. Correctly so: internal /s/-final rhymes cannot exceed the three-segment maximum.

Having dealt with this matter, we may proceed most expeditiously if we now demolish a straw man. Consider the fact that /s/ not only is peculiar in rhymes but also exhibits unique behavior in onsets: among nonpalatal obstruents, only /s/ cannot occur before a liquid. Now, we would like to subsume as much as possible of the peculiar behavior of /s/ under a unified account. It would therefore be attractive to attempt to regularize onsets and rhymes simultaneously by allowing *s*-plus-liquid onsets and then shifting the /s/ to the preceding rhyme by means of a special rule that would convert, say, (2.16a) to (2.16b).

(2.16) a. * i sl a   b. is l a

          ROR   ROR

Unfortunately, this plan won't work. First, there exist many well-formed words like *austral,* in which the relevant onset is already maximal without /s/:

(2.17) austral

R O

There is thus no source for the /s/ of the preceding rhyme—unless the structure of onsets is redesigned ad hoc to allow inclusion of /s/, an obviously wrong move. Second, there are well-formed words like *vals, Max = Ma*[ks], *ónix = óni*[ks], etc., with an /s/ in word-final position that has no other possible source.

In short, there seems to be no alternative to the following rule:

(2.18) *Rhyme Rule R3*
    Adjoin the segment /s/ to the right of an existing rhyme.

Rule R3 adds the following structure to the inventory of Spanish rhymes:

(2.19)

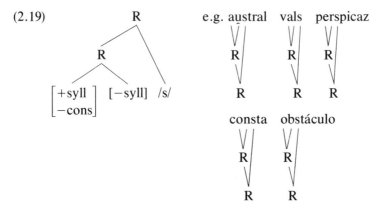

Rule R3 is the first of the proposed syllable-structure-building rules that must refer to features other than [syllabic] and [consonantal], that is, the first one that must make reference to other than major classes of segments. It is thus evidently a highly marked rule, which accords well with the uniqueness of the behavior of /s/.

Our earlier attempt to subsume more than one peculiar property of /s/ under a single generalization did not succeed. There is, however, another idiosyncrasy of /s/ that does not follow directly from rule R3 but is related to it. Consider the following set of examples, which can be extended ad libitum:

(2.20) a. hemi/sf/erio → hemi[sf]erio 'hemisphere'
          /sf/era →   [esf]era 'sphere'

      b. yugo/sl/avo → yugo[sl]avo 'Yugoslav'
          /sl/avo   →   [esl]avo 'Slav(ic)'

      c. in/sp/irar → in[sp]irar 'to breathe in'
          /sp/irar →   [esp]irar 'to breathe'

These will be recognized as examples of the familiar process of Spanish *e*-epenthesis, which has traditionally been formulated as shown in (2.21):

(2.21) $\emptyset \rightarrow$ e / # ____ s [+consonantal]

Improvements on this tradition are suggested in Harris (1980). I propose there that the structural change of (2.21) consists of the insertion of an empty [+syllabic] position into the prosodic skeleton. This position is subsequently assigned the value [e] by an independently motivated rule that applies without contextual restriction. For ease of reference I give this rule as (2.22):

(2.22) V → V
        | |
            e

I now propose to push this line of analysis a step further, in a direction that makes maximal appeal to universal grammar. It is plausible to postulate a universal principle of markedness whose effect can be stated roughly as follows:

(2.23) Insert a vowel before syllabic consonants; that is,

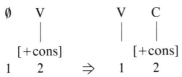

The intention of (2.23) is to assert that syllabic consonants are marked with respect to VC rhymes—surely an uncontroversial proposition. We may now restate the Spanish epenthesis rule (2.21) in the simplest way imaginable:

(2.24) Unattached /s/ becomes syllabic; that is,

$$/s/ \rightarrow /s/$$

```
   |      |
   C      V
   |      |
```

Taking (2.23) and (2.24) into account, we now generate derivations like (2.25):

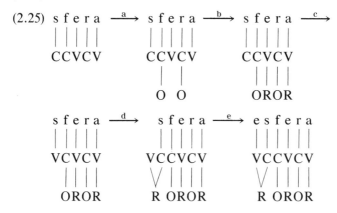

(2.25) s f e r a $\xrightarrow{a}$ s f e r a $\xrightarrow{b}$ s f e r a $\xrightarrow{c}$

```
        | | | | |          | | | | |          | | | | |
        C C V C V          C C V C V          C C V C V
                             | |                | | | |
                             O O                O R O R
```

        s f e r a $\xrightarrow{d}$ s f e r a $\xrightarrow{e}$ e s f e r a

```
        | | | | |          | | | | |          | | | | | |
        V C V C V          V C C V C V         V C C V C V
        | | | |            V | | | |           V | | | |
        O R O R            R O R O R           R O R O R
```

The initial representation in (2.25) shows the segmental string /sfera/ attached to its prosodic skeleton, where C and V stand for [−syllabic] and [+syllabic], respectively. Step (a) is the application of the Onset Rule (2.4). The output shown is the only one possible, since the alternative (2.26) is rejected by a filter to be formulated in section 2.4.

(2.26) *s   f

```
         \ /
          O
```

Step (b) is the application of the basic Rhyme Rule R1.[7] Step (c) illustrates the application of the new formulation (2.24), which makes unattached /s/ syllabic. Step (d) shows the result of principle (2.23). The resulting VC sequence is automatically incorporated into syllable structure by R1, which operates whenever its conditions are met, as do all prosodic structure rules. Finally, step (e) shows the application of the context-free rule (2.22).

We must not be misled into seeing the length of derivation (2.25) as complexity in the technical sense. All of (2.25) is carried out almost automatically, by the interaction of universal principles with a few language-particular rules of great generality and low markedness, as already observed.

Why does (2.24) work? Setting aside the obvious and the irrelevant, the answer is this: we need not specify "in word-initial position" or "before /s/ followed by a [+consonantal] segment" as in (2.21), since /s/ will be "attached," that is, incorporated into syllable structure in all other positions, either as an onset by rule (2.4) or as a rhyme by (2.8) or (2.18).

2.3.5 The Special Case of GVG

Rules R1 and R2 generate GVG rhymes, although (as noted in paragraph (h) below (1.21)) the status of such rhymes is unclear. My decision to treat them as grammatical is based on the following considerations: (a) GVG rhymes do occur in both internal and final rhymes in a handful of actual words, and (b) native speakers' reaction to hypothetical words with GVG rhymes are not decisive one way or the other, in my opinion. This situation is rather different from that of VGC rhymes, which I have considered ill formed. I have been able to find this rhyme type only in internal position and only in four actual words (*aunque, veinte, treinta, auxilio*), and native reaction to hypothetical words containing them is strongly negative. (A typical comment: "¡Horror! ¡¿Cómo puede nadie decir tales cosas?!") I will take these differences as justification for treating GVG and VGC rhymes as grammatical and ungrammatical, respectively, until some more delicate way to tap native judgments can be found or some other type of evidence can be brought to bear on the issue.

2.4 Filters

2.4.1 Onsets

Onset Rule (2.4) of section 2.2, in collaboration with the universal theory of syllable structure, establishes that two-segment onsets in Spanish consist of sequences of the major classes obstruent and liquid, appearing in that order. We must now account for the fact that only certain members of these major classes of segments cooccur, as is illustrated in section 1.2. For convenience, I include here a summary of occurring and nonoccurring clusters:

(2.27) pr/pl   tr/(tl)   *čr/*čl   kr/kl
      br/bl   dr/*dl   (*žr/*žl)   gr/gl
      fr/fl   *sr/*sl   ?xr/?xl

Let us examine first the set of clusters beginning with coronal t and d. As the notation in (2.27) suggests, tr and dr are permissible in all dialects, tl is permissible in some dialects but not others, and dl is disallowed in all dialects. In order to make sense of this distribution, we must be aware of these feature specifications:

(2.28)   t   d   r   l
    continuant[8]   −   −   +   −
    voice   −   +   +   +

Thus, the clusters under discussion are characterized as follows:

(2.29) a. *Allowed:*

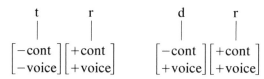

      b. *Allowed ~ Disallowed:*

$$
\begin{array}{cc}
t & l \\
| & | \\
\begin{bmatrix} -\text{cont} \\ -\text{voice} \end{bmatrix} & \begin{bmatrix} -\text{cont} \\ +\text{voice} \end{bmatrix}
\end{array}
$$

      c. *Disallowed:*

$$
\begin{array}{cc}
\overset{.}{d} & l \\
| & | \\
\begin{bmatrix} -\text{cont} \\ +\text{voice} \end{bmatrix} & \begin{bmatrix} -\text{cont} \\ +\text{voice} \end{bmatrix}
\end{array}
$$

We see then that dialects that allow tl as well as tr and dr but exclude dl have filter (2.30):

$$
(2.30) \quad *\left[\begin{bmatrix} +\text{cor} \\ -\text{cont} \\ +\text{voice} \end{bmatrix} \begin{bmatrix} +\text{cor} \\ -\text{cont} \\ +\text{voice} \end{bmatrix} \right]_{\text{Onset}}
$$

Less permissive dialects—those that exclude both tl and dl—have the more general filter (2.31):[9]

(2.31) $*\left[\left[\begin{array}{c}+\text{cor}\\-\text{cont}\end{array}\right]\left[\begin{array}{c}+\text{cor}\\-\text{cont}\end{array}\right]\right]_{\text{Onset}}$

I turn now to the fricative–liquid and affricate–liquid clusters, which are listed again for convenience in (2.32). Clusters with $\check{z}$ are parenthesized since this segment does not occur at all in most dialects.[10]

(2.32) fr   *sr   *čr   (*žr)   ?xr
        fl   *sl   *čl   (*žl)   ?xl

There is no doubt about the status of *fr, fl* on the one hand and of *sr, *sl, *čr, *čl* on the other. The former occur freely, while the latter are utterly beyond the pale in Spanish. (Incidentally, *čl* is already ruled out as an accidental by-product of (2.30) and (2.31), a fact which seems to have no interesting consequences.) The status of *xr, xl*, however, is obscure. They are easily pronounceable in nonce forms (in vivid contrast to *sr, *sl, *čr, *čl*) but are found in no native words and in only one foreign word of any currency, namely, *Jruschef* = [xruščef].[11] Are clusters with [x] well formed or not? As is prudent in such cases, we will let the grammar decide for us. We can do this by setting the questionable cases aside temporarily while we seek a persuasive generalization that makes the right decisions in all of the clear cases. We then see what this generalization says about the clusters with [x]. The clusters we must scrutinize are the following:

(2.33) dr   tr   *sr   *čr
        (tl) *sl   *čl

The generalization is obvious to students of Spanish phonetics: *t* and *d* are literally "dental" (that is, articulated at the inner face of the upper incisors), while *r, l, s, č* are literally "alveolar" (that is, articulated at or behind the alveolar ridge (Navarro Tomás (1965, 65–127))). Unfortunately, it is controversial at present what distinctive features represent this distinction. But we cannot allow a theoretical uncertainty to prevent us from stating a transparent generalization, namely, that clusters whose members differ in "alveolarity" are permissible (*tr, dr, tl*), while those whose members both have this property are ungrammatical (*sr, *sl, *čr, *čl, *žr, *žl*). Thus, all dialects of Spanish are subject to the following filter:

(2.34) $*[[+\text{alveolar}][+\text{alveolar}]]_{\text{onset}}$

Filter (2.34) does not affect *pr, pl, br, bl, kr, kl, gr, gl*, whose first members are noncoronal and hence necessarily nonalveolar. The same is true of *xr, xl*, which we therefore take to be well formed though missing in native words.

2.4.2 Rhymes

As pointed out in section 1.4, there is only one cooccurrence restriction on the elements of otherwise well-formed rhymes, namely, that sequences of high [−consonantal] segments that agree in backness (or roundness) are prohibited:

(2.35) *ii̯   *i̯i   *u̯u   *uu̯

Actually, this is merely a special case of a more general observation that I have so far not made explicit: Spanish does not have long vowels.[12] Assuming, as all recent studies of prosodic structure have done, that long vowels are correctly represented as sequences of [−consonantal] positions in the prosodic skeleton, then this general property of Spanish rhymes can be expressed by the following filter:

$$(2.36) \quad *\left[X \begin{bmatrix} -\text{consonantal} \\ \alpha F \end{bmatrix} \begin{bmatrix} -\text{consonantal} \\ \alpha F \end{bmatrix} Y\right]_{\text{Rhyme}}$$

Here [αF] is shorthand for the features [high], [back], and [round]; the variables X, Y take into account the fact that Spanish rhymes may exceed two segments in length.

Actually, filter (2.36) presumably costs nothing in the grammar of Spanish. No language has ever been described as having only long vowels; thus, if a language has long vowels at all, it also has short vowels. This implication is tantamount to saying that long vowels are marked with respect to short vowels. Therefore, a language-particular statement allowing long vowels should have a cost attached to it, but one forbidding them should not.

2.4.3 Filters as Dissimilarity Requirements

All of the filters (2.30), (2.31), (2.34), and (2.36) share the property of requiring some dissimilarity between the members of a cluster. To attribute to chance the appearance of this property in four filters in a single language would presumably strain most linguists' tolerance for coincidence, as it does mine. However, further discussion of the matter must await investigation of other languages along the lines pursued here for Spanish. The following section carries forward the issue of the nature and role of filters.

2.5 The Erasure Convention

Consider these examples:

(2.37) a. escu/lp/ + ir   → escu[lp]ir   'to sculpt'
       escu/lp/ + tura   → escu[l]tura   'sculpture'
       escu/lp/ + tor   → escu[l]tor   'sculptor'

    b. disti/ng/ + ir   → disti[ŋg]ir   'to distinguish'
       disti/ng/ + ción → disti[n]ción   'distinction'
       disti/ng/ + to   → disti[n]to   'distinct'

Harris (1969, 141–142) accounts for the phenomenon illustrated in (2.37) with a rule of Cluster Simplification: a stop between a consonant and another obstruent is deleted.

I can now suggest another, better, approach. Notice that the medial cluster of *escu*/lpt/*or, disti*/ngt/*o,* etc., cannot be parsed by syllable-structure-assigning rules. The clusters *lpt, ngt* are neither possible onsets nor possible rhymes, and they cannot be divided into a possible rhyme followed by a possible onset. Thus, the assignment of syllable structure (to the substrings in question) can go just this far:

(2.38) a. esculptor   b. distingto
       \\/ | \\/ |
       R O   R O

Unattached *p, g* can never be incorporated. I propose, then, that the correct surface representations *escu*[lt]*or, disti*[nt]*o,* etc., are produced not by a deletion rule but by the following convention:

(2.39) *Erasure Convention*
    Segments not incorporated into syllable structure at the end of a derivation are erased.

The argument in favor of the Erasure Convention over the deletion rule proposed in Harris (1969) is elementary. The environment of Cluster Simplification must duplicate conditions on syllable structure. Given that syllable structure rules are independently needed, the Cluster Simplification rule is otiose (but the converse does not hold). Furthermore, the Erasure Convention is proposed as a principle of universal grammar, a status that Cluster Simplification obviously cannot attain (cf. English *scu*[lpč]*ure*, *disti*[ŋkš]*ion*, etc.).

The following example illustrates the interaction of the Erasure Convention with a filter. Consider these words, which are representative of a large number of cases:

(2.40) a. copl + a   'ballad'   b. copi̱ + a   'copy'
       copl + ista 'balladeer'   cop + ista 'copyist'

Copla and *copi̱a* consist of the stems *copl-* and *copi̱-* plus the *terminal element -a*. Why is the final segment of the stem lost in *copista* (**copi̱ista*) but not in *coplista*? The former is the interesting case. Here, the application of syllable structure rules (to the substring in question) can proceed no farther than (2.41),

(2.41) copi̱ista
       | \/
       O R

since filter (2.36), which excludes adjacent nonconsonantal segments in a rhyme if these segments agree in height and frontness, blocks incorporation of the remaining glide *i̱* by rule R2 into an otherwise well-formed rhyme. This segment is then disposed of by the Erasure Convention. We can also do away with a rule of "like vowel deletion" proposed in Harris (1980c), which is now superfluous for reasons analogous to those just given in connection with the Cluster Simplification rule.

In sum, the descriptive advantage afforded by the Erasure Convention is that it allows a unified account of phenomena that were previously seen as consequences of unrelated rules of segmental phonology—rules, furthermore, that duplicate the effects of syllable structure conditions.

Sometimes initially unparsable strings are "rescued" by independently motivated phonological rules. We saw one example of this in (2.25) of section 2.3.4. Recall that in this case an originally stranded word-initial /s/ is incorporated into a rhyme as in (2.42), which protects the /s/ from the Erasure Convention.

(2.42) e s

       R

The following examples illustrate another case:

(2.43) a/br/ + ir   → a[β r]ir   'to open'
      a/br/ + tura → a[βer]tura 'opening'

The medial cluster of a/brt/ura cannot be parsed by syllable structure rules. We might therefore expect the eventual operation of the Erasure Convention to produce *a[βt]ura, or something of the sort; however, this result is circumvented as follows:

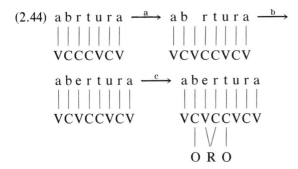

(2.44) a b r t u r a $\xrightarrow{a}$ a b   r t u r a $\xrightarrow{b}$
       VCCCVCV   VCVCCVCV

       a b e r t u r a $\xrightarrow{c}$ a b e r t u r a
       VCVCCVCV   VCVCCVCV
                              O R O

Step (a) shows the effect of a rule that inserts a [+syllabic] position in the prosodic skeleton in the environment C ____ rC. (There are no surface occurrences of CrC in Spanish; cf. Harris (1977b, 274–275) for additional discussion.) Step (b) is the operation of rule (2.22), which associates e with an empty V position in the prosodic skeleton. Finally step (c) shows the application of familiar onset and rhyme structure rules. Ultimately, then, it is step (a) that saves the originally interconsonantal r from elimination by the Erasure Convention.

To close this section, I will present a case in which the Erasure Convention has the effect of a constraint on the lexicon. Consider the following array of data:

(2.45)

	$V(C) + o\#$	$V(C) + a\#$	$V(C) + e\#$	$V(C)\#$
a. -$V(V)$	mo(h)o	anchoa	oboe	caló
-$Vr(V)$	cero	cera	ere	mujer
-$Vl(V)$	polo	amapola	mole	bemol
-$Vn(V)$	heno	pena	pene	pan
-$Vd(V)$	dedo	seda	sede	sed
-$Vt(V)$	bruto	fruta	matute	mamut
-$Vs(V)$	paso	pasa	pase	compás
-$Vk(V)$	pico	chica	dique	tic
-$V[x](V)$	espejo	reja	eje	reloj
-$Vy(V)$	leguleyo	epopeya	muelle	buey

(2.45) b.	-Gs(V)	aplauso	causa	sauce	seis
	-Cs(V)	falso	salsa	embalse	vals
	-Os(V)	lapso	laxa	eclipse	bíceps
c.	-GL(V)	centauro	aula	baile	*
	-GN(V)	reino	reina	peine	*
	-GO(V)	mosaico	gaita	naipe	*
	-LG(V)	serio	miseria	serie	*
	-NG(V)	genio	venia	progenie	*
	-OG(V)	vicio	caricia	calvicie	*
	-LN(V)	enfermo	merma	uniforme	*
	-NN(V)	himno	columna	solemne	*
	-ON(V)	fresno	cuaresma	cisne	*
	-LO(V)	parto	carta	parte	*
	-NO(V)	canto	santa	guante	*
	-OO(V)	pacto	acta	traste	*

The words in (2.45) are nouns and adjectives. The word-final vowels
-o, -a, -e in the first three columns are *terminal elements,* which are the
outermost morphological units possible in an uninflected noun or adjective. The existence of words of type V(C)# in (2.45a,b) versus the
nonexistence of words of the same type in (2.45c) illustrates the following facts about the lexicon of Spanish. In the general case, noun and
adjective stems are followed by one of the terminal elements -o, -a, -e,
or by no terminal element, as a lexical idiosyncrasy of individual
items.[13] But in one special case (namely, (2.45c)), a terminal element
must appear. At this point we are easily able to characterize independently the relevant difference between the two sets of stems. The stems
of the words in (2.45a,b) end in possible rhymes; those in (2.45c) do
not. It is clear then why no words fill the rightmost column of (2.45c):
they could not surface intact, since their final rhymes would be de-
stroyed by the Erasure Convention.

2.6 On the Descriptive Apparatus

The descriptive devices that have been employed in the foregoing sections imply a fairly rich and eclectic general theory of syllable structure which draws on many of the elements that have been proposed
by other investigators of prosodic structure. The following points are
illustrative:

(a) The proposal that syllable structure is hierarchical (as opposed to the "linear" structures of Hooper (1976), for example) enjoys a tradition that goes back at least to Pike and Pike (1947).

(b) The hypothesis that prosodic structure is (maximally) binary took root in Liberman and Prince (1977) and has been investigated intensively in Hayes (1979, 1980) and other works.

(c) The role of the strong/weak relation in binary trees is crucial in Liberman and Prince (1977) and has been a prominent feature in many subsequent studies, especially Kiparsky (1979).

(d) The sonority scale, which has venerable roots, is a central element in the theories of Hooper (1976), Kiparsky (1979), and others.

(e) The notion of the prosodic skeleton, already implicit in Goldsmith (1976a), is the mainstay of McCarthy (1979a,b) and is explored further in Halle and Vergnaud (1980, forthcoming) and in many other studies.

(f) The proposal that "unattached" or "stranded" segments are not realized phonetically—formulated above as the Erasure Convention—has figured implicitly or explicitly in virtually every work involving the autosegmental approach to phonology.

(g) The distinction between "rules" and "filters" derives most immediately from Fudge's (1969) distinction between "colligational" and "collocational" restrictions.

(h) The proposal that intrasyllabic constituents have category labels is taken immediately from investigations in the line of Halle and Vergnaud, but it has antecedents, notably Saporta and Contreras (1962) and Pike and Pike (1947).

Some of the features of (a) through (h) restrict rather than expand the expressive power of linguistic descriptions. One example is the binarity hypothesis (cf. note 1). Still, the range of devices employed in the present study presupposes a powerful theoretical arsenal. It is accordingly not surprising that these mechanisms make possible the formulation of far-reaching generalizations regarding the structure of Spanish syllables. By the same token, it is imperative to ask whether significant constraints can be imposed on the theoretical model without sacrificing any of our putative insights into the structure of Spanish.

For the most part, I have been fairly explicit about the work done by the theoretical machinery assumed here. For example, I have explained at several points how the proposals of Kiparsky (1979) (integrating binary-branching trees, the strong/weak relation, the sonority scale, and certain conditions of simplicity and maximality, etc.) function as a theory of markedness which allows us to see certain properties

of Spanish (e.g., the order of consonants in two-segment onsets) as
"natural" and thus not requiring language-particular statements for
their expression.

The role of some other elements is more or less self-evident. For
example, it is presumably not necessary to spell out in further detail
how the device of filters pays its way by excluding certain terminal
sequences allowed by the most general statement of the syllable-
building rules.

No doubt the least well motivated device at this point is the node
labels O and R—though the legitimacy of the constituents themselves
that are so labeled does not seem to be open to serious question. We
have seen so far that these constituents—which I will continue to call
onset and *rhyme* for convenience even while questioning the theoretical
significance of the labels—have different internal arrangements. For
example, rhymes may contain glides but onsets cannot, permissible
consonant clusters in onsets are not just mirror images of those allowed
in rhymes (OL in onsets but *LO in rhymes, Cs in rhymes but *sC in
onsets), etc. Structure-building rules must thus be able to distinguish
between "onsets" and "rhymes," and it is not obvious that there is a
better way to do it than to provide distinct labels for them, say, O and
R. Evidence that is perhaps more persuasive appears in chapter 3,
where we will see several generalizations of the following form:

(2.46) x → y / ____

$$\begin{array}{c}\rule{1.5em}{0.4pt}\\ |\\ R\end{array}$$

That is, something happens to a segment just in case it is in a rhyme,
regardless of its position in the rhyme (e.g., regardless of whether it is
rhyme-final or followed by another segment). It is not obvious that
there exists a viable alternative to specifying the label R in such rules.
Consider the following.[14] Suppose that *x* is a segment that appears in
both of the structures (2.47a,b) and is changed to *y* in both:

(2.47) a. V   x   b. V   x   s

Of course rule (2.46) gives the desired results if all of the nodes in (2.47)
are labeled R. Now assume that syllabic node labels other than σ do
not exist. Rule (2.46) is reformulated as follows:

(2.48) $x \rightarrow y /$ ____ $]_\sigma$

Now observe that if rule (2.48) is allowed to apply *between* rule R1 and rule R3 (both suitably reformulated), the desired output *Vys* can be produced:

(2.49) V x s $\xrightarrow{\text{R1}}$ V x s $\xrightarrow{(2.48)}$ V y s $\xrightarrow{\text{R3}}$ V y s

Let us evaluate this proposal. Notice first that derivation (2.49) supposes a Theory T_1 which allows intermingling of prosodic-structure-building rules (R1, R3) with segmental-feature-changing rules (2.48), but does not allow node labels except σ. It is hardly obvious a priori that T_1 is more restrictive than a theory T_2 that strictly orders these classes of rules but allows the node labels O and R in addition to σ. Add to this the apparent necessity for including these labels in the structure-building rules themselves (see immediately above), and we do not have a strong presumptive case for T_1, to say the least.

It is not hard to invent a hypothetical but plausible set of data that would favor T_2 over T_1. Suppose (a) that the generalization expressed by (2.46)/(2.48) requires further that the vowel immediately preceding its rhyme-mate x be stressed, and (b) that the rules for stress assignment depend on prior application of all syllable structure rules. The required order of all relevant rules would then be (R1, R3, stress, (2.46)). The derivation in (2.49) would thus be impossible, and the empirically correct grammar would be consistent with T_2 but not with T_1. So far as I can tell, Spanish does not provide a real example of the required form, but some of the material to be presented in chapter 3 comes so close as to suggest that the search will not go unrewarded.

To summarize, no a priori argument seems to be available that would settle the issue of the theoretical status of syllabic constituent labels other than σ. This appears to be a genuine empirical question, although Spanish may not provide crucial evidence. This issue will no doubt be the subject of continuing debate.

The phrase structure grammar model of the analysis of Saporta and Contreras (1962) (which enjoys no little descriptive success) grants theoretical recognition to four syllabic node labels: *S(yllable)*, *O(nset)*,

N(ucleus), and *C(oda)*. I have argued above (especially in section 1.1) that in certain respects this grammar imposes too little structure, namely, by not uniting N and C into a superordinate rhyme constituent (labeled as such or not). It can also be argued that in other respects Saporta and Contreras's grammar imposes too much structure. Specifically, no known generalization of Spanish requires recognition of separate "nucleus" and "coda" constituents (so labeled or not) within the "rhyme"; furthermore, setting up these rhyme-internal constituents results in empirically incorrect predictions.

Disregarding a number of refinements that are not relevant in the present context, Saporta and Contreras's grammar assigns the following constituency to post-onset segments:

(2.50)

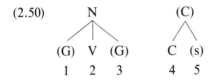

(The numbering is for reference only; it is not a part of the grammar.) Although Saporta and Contreras do not say so explicitly, their intention seems to be to capture the generalization that the (obligatory) nucleus and the (optional) coda contain only [−consonantal] and [+consonantal] segments, respectively. (N and C play no other discernible role.) On close examination, however, this generalization turns out to be dysfunctional. The fact is that the nucleus-final glide position 3 and the coda-initial consonant position 4 are mutually exclusive: as we have seen, (G)VGC(s) rhymes are ill formed. Furthermore, allowing both of these positions incorrectly predicts the existence of rhymes two segments longer than the now familiar maximum of three. I have argued above, in essence, that Saporta and Contreras's positions 3 and 4 are actually a single [−syllabic] slot in the prosodic template. This simultaneously accounts for the mutual exclusivity of glides and consonants following position 2 and reduces the overall excess length to one segment (allowing for the formulation of a presumably more natural additional stipulation to bar the unwanted segment).

In short, the known evidence weighs against (2.50). I conclude at this stage of investigation that the intrasyllabic node labels which can be motivated in Spanish are at best O(nset) and R(hyme).

2.7 Resyllabification

In practically any elementary treatise on Spanish pronunciation, a statement can be found to the effect that syllable boundaries do not necessarily coincide with word boundaries. More precisely, in casual speech a word-final consonant syllabifies with the initial vowel of the following word. For example:

(2.51) Los otros estaban en el avión.

'The others were on the airplane.'

Resyllabification requires that the second word start with a vowel; final consonants will not link with a nonvowel even though the cluster that would result is permissible within a word:

(2.52) club lindo ↛ *club lindo   *but*   blindo

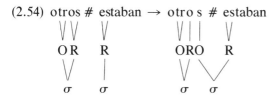

The string on which resyllabification operates is thus precisely:

(2.53) [+cons] # V

Example (2.54) illustrates the change in syllable structure:

(2.54) otros # estaban → otro s # estaban

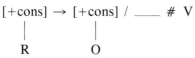

This change can be viewed as follows. We stipulate that a rule, to be called Resyllabification, changes the labeling of a word-final consonant from R to O in the relevant environment:

(2.55) *Resyllabification*

$$[+\text{cons}] \rightarrow [+\text{cons}] / \underline{\quad} \# \text{ V}$$
           R   O

Then independent processes complete the new structure without further stipulation:

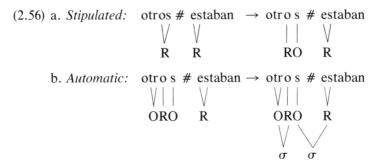

(2.56) a. *Stipulated:*   otros # estaban   → otro s # estaban
b. *Automatic:*   otro s # estaban → otro s # estaban

Observe that Resyllabification, a prosodic process, does not alter syntactic structure. This is reflected in our notation by the fact that Resyllabification does not delete word boundaries. As a result, syllable boundaries and word boundaries need not coincide (as was mentioned at the beginning of this section), and (syntactic) words need not be comprised of an integral number of (prosodic) syllables.[15]

Resyllabification, in conjunction with the structures discussed in previous sections, can contribute to an improved understanding of several problems in Spanish phonology, to which we now turn.

Chapter 3
Case Studies

3.1 Aspiration and Velarization

In many dialects, /s/ is aspirated (becomes some kind of *h*), assimilates totally to a following segment, or is deleted altogether, under certain conditions; e.g., *despué*s = *de*[h]*pué*[h]. Another common phenomenon is the velarization or deletion of /n/, under certain conditions, e.g., *cantan* = *ca*[ŋ]*ta*[ŋ]. Both processes are often, but not necessarily, found in the same dialect. My concern here is to characterize correctly the environment in which these processes take place. Thus, for convenience I will refer to them as *aspiration* and *velarization,* and I will write the changes as *s* → *h* and *n* → *ŋ,* despite the fact that neither the terminology nor the symbols do justice to the full range of phonetic detail involved.

Aspiration and velarization, especially the former, have spawned a gargantuan literature in the last decade or so,[1] wherein it is routinely assumed that these phenomena occur precisely in syllable-final position. Guitart (1979, 1980a) has observed perceptively that this assumption is not obviously correct. I borrow his examples:

(3.1) a. i[ŋ]s-tituto
      b. Ramó-[ŋ]entró
         tiene-[h]espacio

In the typical pronunciation of *instituto* suggested in (3.1a), *n* is velarized although the following *s* rather than the *n* itself is in syllable-final position. In (3.1b), *Ramón entró* shows velarization and *tienes espacio* shows aspiration despite the fact that the indicated segments are in syllable-initial position. Guitart concludes that the rules are as shown in (3.2):

(3.2) a. *Velarization*

$$n \rightarrow \text{ŋ} / \underline{} \begin{Bmatrix} C \\ \# \end{Bmatrix}$$

b. *Aspiration*

$$s \rightarrow h / [+\text{sonorant}] \underline{} \begin{Bmatrix} C \\ \# \end{Bmatrix}$$

Although Guitart's observations are accurate and cogent, his conclusion does not follow. There is no obstacle to stating these rules as in (3.3):

(3.3) a. *Velarization*

n → ŋ
|
R

b. *Aspiration*

s → h / [+sonorant] ____
|
R

Example (3.1a) presents no problem, given the syllable structure shown in (3.4a):

(3.4) a. R   b.   R

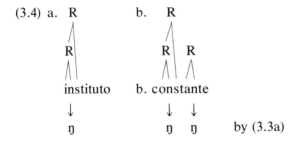

instituto   b. constante
    ↓   ↓   ↓
    ŋ   ŋ   ŋ   by (3.3a)

I include *constante* simply to illustrate the velarization of *n* in (literally) syllable-final position.

The cases in (3.1b) are also readily accounted for, as shown in (3.5), where the left-to-right arrow indicates application of Resyllabification after application of Velarization and Aspiration (3.3a,b):

(3.5) a.

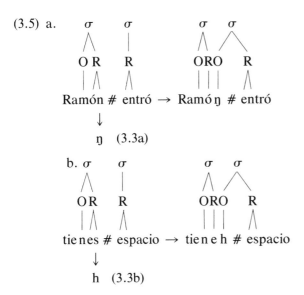

Ramón # entró → Ramó ŋ # entró
↓
ŋ   (3.3a)

b.   tienes # espacio → tiene h # espacio
↓
h   (3.3b)

It is hard to imagine that rules (3.3a,b) could be considered less descriptively adequate than rules (3.2a,b) with their disjunctive environment. Indeed, (3.5) captures a generalization that a grammar containing (3.2a,b) necessarily misses: velarized *n* and aspirated *s* occur in syllable-initial position only if they are also in word-final position and followed by a word that begins with a vowel, i.e., precisely in the environment of Resyllabification.[2]

3.2 "Liquid Gliding" in Cibaeño

In Cibaeño Spanish,[3] the liquids *r* and *l* are optionally realized as [i̯] under certain conditions.[4] Following Guitart (1980b), I refer to this phenomenon as *liquid gliding*. Examples follow:

(3.6) revolver = revo[i̯]ve[i̯]
      carta   = ca[i̯]ta
      papel   = pape[i̯]
      algo   = a[i̯]go

On the basis of simple data such as these we would conclude that liquid gliding takes place in syllable-final position, or more accurately—assuming that words like *pers-pectiva* can be pronounced *pe*[i̯]*s-pectiva*—in rhymes:

(3.7) L → i̯
       |
       R

There are some complications, however. Consider the following representative examples:

(3.8)   *Before C*   *Before V*
a. papel blanco = pape[i̯]   papel azul   = pape[i̯] azul
   'white paper'   blanco   'blue paper'
   él da   = é[i̯] da   él avisa   = é[i̯] avisa
   'he gives'   'he advises'

b. el día   = e[i̯] día   el aviso   = e[l] aviso
   'the day'   'the advice'

Surprisingly, liquid gliding does not occur in the case illustrated by *el aviso*. It seems, then, that liquid gliding occurs word-finally in oxytones regardless of what follows (3.8a); but in unstressed monosyllables—which include the constractions *al* and *del* and the preposition *por* in addition to the article *el*—liquid gliding occurs preceding a consonant but not a vowel (3.8b). This complex statement describes the data accurately, but it is ad hoc and unrevealing.

Guitart (1980b) undertakes to provide a principled description of liquid gliding, including the odd data of (3.8). He proposes first that rather than position in the syllable, "the true environment for liquid gliding is actually the disjunction shown in [(3.9)]" (1980b, 7):

(3.9) / ___ $\begin{Bmatrix} C \\ \# \end{Bmatrix}$

Guitart then suggests that "articles and prepositions do not have word status but are perhaps clitics," and that the boundary between a clitic and the following word is not word boundary (#) but rather "morpheme boundary (+), whose presence does not trigger the gliding process" (1980b, 8). According to these proposals, then, the contrast between *él avisa* 'he advises' and *el aviso* 'the advice', for example, arises as follows:

(3.10) a. /el # avisa/   b. /el + aviso/
          i̯   –   L → i̯ / ___ {C,#}
       é[i̯] *avísa*   e[l] *avíso*   surface forms

The analysis just sketched, with its explicit and crucial reliance on the environment (3.9), constitutes a direct challenge to the claim that analyses that depend on this environment can always be reformulated with equal or greater descriptive adequacy in terms of syllable structure (see the introduction). This challenge can be met, and met on the basis of Guitart's own perceptive observations and suggestions. We need only provide a reinterpretation of the clitic status of the unstressed monosyllables illustrated in (3.8b).

The word *clitic* is as much a prosodic term as a syntactic one. In the case at hand, the syntactic structure and prosodic structure are linked as follows (W = "prosodic word"). (See Selkirk (1978, in preparation) for general discussion.)

(3.11)

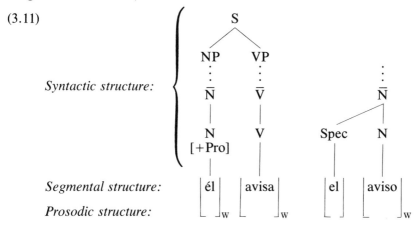

It is within prosodic structure, not syntactic structure, that the domain of prosodic phenomena like stress and syllabification is staked out. Derivations like the following thus arise, where the domain of (3.12a,b) is [...]$_W$:[5]

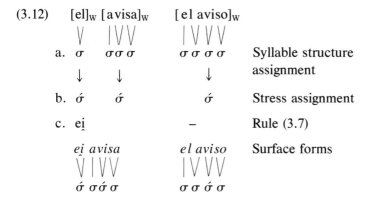

In sum, as (3.11) and (3.12) show, Guitart's correct observation regarding the status of *el*, *por*, etc., as clitics, when given an interpretation in prosodic terms, provides the basis for a principled answer to his question. The theoretical challenge is thus met, unless an argument can be made that the analysis outlined in (3.11) and (3.12) constitutes a description inferior to the one proposed in Guitart (1980b). I do not believe that such an argument can be constructed. In any event, the onus of proof rests on opponents of (3.11)–(3.12), since this analysis is framed in the more restrictive and hence a priori more desirable theory that eschews the environment of (3.9).

3.3 Lateral and Nasal Depalatalization

Section 2.7 demonstrated that the process of resyllabification produces cyclic effects in reassigning syllable structure across word boundaries. In this section we will see that "syllable structure assignment is cyclic" within words as well.[6] The two sets of cyclic effects are not identical, however, as I will show later.

3.3.1 Lateral Depalatalization
The palatal segment represented by orthographic *ll* alternates with nonpalatal [l] in many words, a phenomenon that I will refer to as *Lateral Depalatalization*. Examples follow:

(3.13) a. va<u>ll</u>e   Va<u>l</u>derrobles   'valley'   'Valley of Oaks'
         be<u>ll</u>o   be<u>l</u>dad   'beautiful'   'beauty'

       b. donce<u>ll</u>a   donce<u>l</u>   'lass'   'lad'
          e<u>ll</u>a   é<u>l</u>   'she'   'he'

These cases show *ll* alternating with [l] before a consonant and in word-final position, respectively. It is thus not without reason that Contreras (1977, 11–13) has written the following rule:[7]

(3.14) $$L \rightarrow l \; / \; \underline{\hspace{1cm}} \begin{Bmatrix} C \\ \# \end{Bmatrix}$$

This rule presents a challenge analogous to the one successfully met in the previous section, namely, to justify restatement of (3.14) as (3.15):

(3.15) L → 1

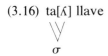

R

The present task of reanalysis is somewhat tricky, because Lateral Depalatalization seems to be doubly opaque.

On the one hand, the palatal lateral [ʎ] can apparently occur in syllable-final position in such an utterance as *tal llave* 'such a key', if pronounced as (3.16).

(3.16) ta[ʎ] llave

σ

(Such a case renders (3.14) opaque no less than (3.15).) Here the final *l* of *tal* is assimilated by a low-level rule to the initial palatal of the following word (Harris (1969, 18–20)). This assimilation differs from depalatalization in the following ways: (a) the assimilation is an optional fast-speech phenomenon, while depalatalization is obligatory and independent of style in all dialects; (b) the assimilation produces [ʎ] in dialects in which the L of (3.14) and (3.15) is never realized as [ʎ]. Clearly, then, the two processes are distinct, and the presumed existence of the assimilation process casts no doubt on the correctness of (3.15).

Lateral Depalatalization is opaque in the other direction in that cases exist in which it appears to have operated in syllable-initial position. These more interesting cases are illustrated in (3.17):

(3.17) a. donceLas   b. donce l es

OR   OR

Doncellas, donceles are the plurals of the first set of examples in (3.13b). The syllable structure of *donceles* is the same as that of *doncellas*. Why not *doncelles*? That is, how has Lateral Depalatalization applied to produce the *l* of *donceles* in syllable-initial position? An answer comes to light when we consider the morphological structure of these words:

(3.18)   *Singular*   *Plural*
Masculine   [doncel]ₙ   [[doncel]ₙ es]ₙ
Feminine   [doncell + a]ₙ   [[doncell + a]ₙ s]ₙ

The -*a*- of *doncella(s)* is the *terminal element,* often correlated with feminine gender, which is absent in masculine *doncel.* There is nothing controversial about the morphological structure displayed in (3.18).[8]

Now, taking the underlying representation of the root to be /doncelL-/, we may propose a derivation for *donceles* that includes the following steps:

(3.19) *Inner cycle:*

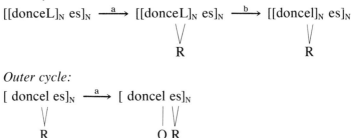

Outer cycle:

Step (a) in the inner cycle is syllable structure assignment; step (b) is the operation of Lateral Depalatalization (3.15) on the basis of the structure assigned in step (a). Step (a) in the outer cycle is really the same as in the inner cycle: the newly available segments are incorporated into the syllable structure of the word. Lateral Depalatalization (3.15) applies when its structural description is met, namely, in the first cycle, after syllable structure has been assigned.

Lateral Depalatalization is obviously an obligatory neutralization rule. This places it in the class of cyclic rules, according to Mascaró (1976). It applies to *doncel* on the first cycle, since—as just mentioned—it is (intrinsically) fed by Syllable Structure Assignment, which creates a derived environment. Thus, in order to achieve the results shown in (3.19) without ad hoc stipulations, we need only officially recognize [...]ₙ as a cyclic domain.[9]

3.3.2 Nasal Depalatalization
The palatal nasal *ñ* = [ɲ] alternates under certain circumstances with nonpalatal *n,* a phenomenon I will refer to as *Nasal Depalatalization.* Examples follow:

(3.20) a. reñir   rencilla   'to quarrel'   'quarrel' (noun)
       b. desdeñar   desdén   'to disdain'   'disdain' (noun)
          doña   don   (as in *doña Elvira, don Juan*)

These examples show ñ alternating with *n* before a consonant and in word-final position, respectively. Thus, Contreras (1977, 13–14) proposes that the rule of Nasal Depalatalization has the environment shown in (3.21):

(3.21) ñ → n / ___ $\left\{\begin{array}{l} C \\ \# \end{array}\right\}$

As before, I will take up the challenge to justify restating this rule as follows:

(3.22) ñ → n
        |
        R

   Nasal Depalatalization is obviously quite similar to Lateral Depalatalization, but with a few special features of its own. Because of these I refrain from formulating the two processes as a single rule.[10] The most obvious difference is that while the phonetic realizations of orthographic *ll* vary radically, as has been pointed out, ñ is always [ñ] in all dialects.
   Nasal Depalatalization is opaque in the same way as Lateral Depalatalization, only more so. Palatal [ñ] can apparently occur in syllable-final position over a word boundary as a result of a low-level assimilation rule (Harris (1969, 8–18)); e.g., *un ñame* 'a yam' can be *u*[ñ] *ñame*, at least optionally in some dialects. Furthermore, within a word the effect of Nasal Depalatalization is always masked in the environment / ___ C by obligatory Nasal Assimilation (Harris (1969, 8–18; forthcoming)). Thus, it is moot whether the [n] of, say, *rencilla* (3.20a) is the result of Nasal Depalatalization or Nasal Assimilation. This is true whether the rule is stated as in (3.21) or as in (3.22). By the same token, a case like (3.23) contributes equally to the opacity of the two formulations.

(3.23) cónyuge = có[ñ]yuge
                     | |
                     R O

Nasal Depalatalization is opaque in the other direction in that cases exist in which the rule appears to have operated in syllable-initial position. The following pair provides an absolutely minimal contrast:

(3.24) a. desdeñes   b. desdenes

      T\/   T\/
      O R   O R

Desdeñes is a verb, meaning 'you disdain', present subjunctive, singular. *Desdenes* is the plural of the noun *desdén* 'disdain' (3.20b). As in the case of *doncellas/donceles,* the key to the contrast between *desdeñes* and *desdenes* lies in morphological structure. The latter pair is more subtle and interesting, however, since the surface morphology of the two words is parallel:

(3.25) a. [desdeñ + es]$_V$ b. [desden + es]$_N$

How is it possible, then, that Nasal Depalatalization has applied in the noun but not in the verb? The noun case is the simpler of the two:

(3.26) *Inner cycle:*

[[desdeñ]$_N$ es]$_N$ $\xrightarrow{\text{a}}$ [[desdeñ]$_N$ es]$_N$ $\xrightarrow{\text{b}}$ [[desden]$_N$ es]$_N$

                          \/   \/
                          R   R

   Outer cycle:

[desden es]$_N$ $\xrightarrow{\text{a}}$ [desden es]$_N$

  \/ | \/
  R   O R

Step (a) is again syllable structure assignment, and step (b) is Nasal Depalatalization. Comparison of (3.19) and (3.26) reveals that the two derivations are entirely analogous. All of the remarks made about (3.19) carry over completely to (3.26), and I will not repeat them here.

  The derivation of *desdeñes* includes the following steps:

(3.27) *First (only) cycle:*

[(desdeñ + a)$_V$ e s]$_V$ $\xrightarrow{\text{a}}$ [desdeñ + e + s]$_V$ $\xrightarrow{\text{b}}$

[desdeñ + e + s]$_V$

     | \/
     O   R

In the initial representation of (3.27), (desdeñ + a)ᵥ is the lexical entry of the verb stem, a morphological constituent which I will call the *derivational stem*. The vowel *a* inside the derivational stem is the verbal *theme vowel,* and the *e* outside this stem is the marker of present subjunctive. The rightmost *-s* is the morpheme indicating second person singular. Step (a) in (3.27) shows the morphological operation internal to the lexicon in which the theme vowel is deleted; step (b) is syllable structure assignment. The crucial point here is that in this one-cycle derivation, root-final palatal *ñ* is followed by a vowel at every step. It is thus always in the onset of its syllable, with the consequence that Nasal Depalatalization never has a chance to apply to it.

Stated informally, the essential difference between (3.19) and (3.26) on the one hand, and (3.27) on the other, is that the singular nouns are words, available for lexical insertion. The same is obviously true of plural nouns, but plurals *contain* singulars and thus have two cycles. Nonderived verbs like *desdeñes,* on the other hand, are available for lexical insertion only when their stems are provided with inflections; hence, their derivation involves only one cycle.

The morphological structure illustrated in (3.27) is a familiar one in the literature on Spanish morphology of the last three decades.[11] This fact, coupled with the foregoing remarks concerning (3.19) and (3.26), which carry over completely to (3.27) (mutatis mutandis), makes further discussion of (3.27) unnecessary. In short, the novelty of (3.26) and (3.27) is the way in which independently known morphological structure, interacting with general principles of phonological theory, is brought to bear in the explication of the apparently baffling contrast seen in forms like *desdeñes* versus *desdenes:* this morphological structure determines the application of the rule of Nasal Depalatalization (3.22), given that [...]ₙ and [...]ᵥ are cyclic domains, but (...)ᵥ is not.

In the following section I will examine other data in which cyclic assignment of syllable structure is crucial.

3.4 Syllable Structure Assignment versus Resyllabification; Glide–Consonant Alternations

The previous section illustrated derivations in which syllable structure is adjusted when segments from an outer cycle are incorporated into existing structure. This device is needed independently of the rules of Lateral and Nasal Depalatalization, for example, in the simplest possible case of a plural noun:

(3.28)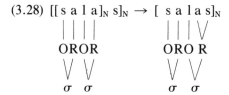

The redrawing of syllable structure in all of these cases evidently results from the interaction of principles of universal syllable theory with
the language-particular morphological structures of Spanish. (See the
arguments for the cyclic nature of syllable structure assignment in
Kiparsky (1979).)

The word-internal reassignment of syllable structure that we have
just been discussing is a phenomenon distinct from resyllabification,
discussed in section 2.7. As noted there, resyllabification is a restricted
process in the sense that it "refuses" to create certain types of syllables
that are well formed within a word (cf. (2.52) in particular). Another
difference is that word-internal reassignment may operate "leftward"
while resyllabification cannot. "*Leftward*" refers to the kind of incorporation shown in (3.28), where the plural marker -*s* is incorporated
into the rhyme to its left. That resyllabification operates only "right-
ward" is demonstrated by the fact that, say, *tiene salas* 'it has rooms'
can be syllabified only as shown in (3.29).

(3.29) tie n e s a las
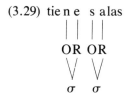

The syllabification that would result from "leftward" resyllabification
is impossible for this phrase:

(3.30) *tie n e s a las
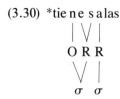

In contrast, the phrase *tienes alas* 'you have wings' has the two possible
syllabifications shown in (3.31):

(3.31) a. tie nes alas   b. tie n e s alas

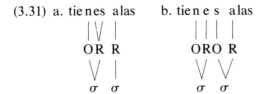

The syllabification (3.31a) is typical of hypercareful pronunciation, in which resyllabification does not occur; (3.31b) is typical of less highly monitored styles, in which resyllabification is the norm. The structure of (3.31a) is of course identical to that of (3.30), which shows that the syllabification itself is well formed, though it cannot arise through the process of resyllabification.

I examine next a long-standing problem of Spanish phonology which can be illuminated by taking into account the fact that word-internal syllable structure adjustment and resyllabification have distinct properties.

All dialects of Spanish have a process whereby the glide [i̯] in a rhyme is changed to a [+consonantal] segment and "promoted" to onset status, under certain conditions. The conditions vary from dialect to dialect, as does the quality of the resulting consonant, which ranges from a lenis voiced *ich-Laut* [ʝ] to the strident affricate [ǰ]. (There is an extensive literature on this subject, which is summarized in Harris (1969, 20–36). See also the references cited there.) To facilitate the exposition here, I will limit attention to the Porteño dialect (spoken in Buenos Aires and environs), which has an obligatory and unmistakable alternation between [i̯] and the strident continuant obstruent [ž]. The following examples illustrate this alternation:

(3.32) convo[i̯]   *vs.* convo[ž]es   'convoy'   'convoys'
       le[i̯]   le[ž]es   'law'   'laws'
(3.33) com[i̯]endo   cre[ž]endo   'eating'   'believing'
       lam[i̯]ó   le[ž]ó   'licked'   'read'

(3.32) presents nouns whose stem ends in [i̯] in the singular but [ž] in the plural. (3.33) illustrates verb inflections whose first segment is [i̯] after a root ending in a consonant (*com-, lam-*) but [ž] after a root ending in a vowel (*cre-, le-*).

Syllable structure plays a crucial role in these data, as (3.34) demonstrates:

(3.34) a. [i̯]   vs.   b. [ž]

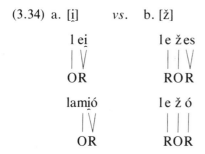

We see in (3.34) that [i̯] and [ž] are in complementary distribution: [i̯] is found in rhymes, before or after the nuclear vowel, while [ž] occurs as an onset. Just this observation, however, is relatively uninformative, since our syllable structure rules already preclude nonconsonantal [i̯] in onsets. More to the point is the fact that the following generalization holds of Porteño Spanish:

(3.35) [i̯] cannot be the first segment in a syllable.

I propose the following rule as the implementation of (3.35) in the grammar of Porteño:

(3.36) i̯ → ž / $_\sigma$[_____   or equivalently   i̯ → ž /

$$\sigma$$

This rule is a striking peculiarity of Porteño. It accounts for the special status of [i̯] as the only segment in Spanish whose realizations vary so radically—from glide to strident obstruent—depending on its position in prosodic structure. As mentioned earlier, other dialects have rules analogous to (3.36) but involving a less extreme change. It should also be mentioned that (3.36) has a handful of lexical exceptions. The exceptionality of particular words varies from speaker to speaker; too, it is apparently on the way out of the language, since words that are exceptional for older speakers are not so for younger speakers. (Cf. Lozano (1979, 33).)

In most cases, the operation of (3.36) is straightforward. Take, for example, the first two words in (3.33):

(3.37) a. σ   σ   b. σ   σ   σ   σ
        ∧ ∕∖   ∧ | ∧   ∧
       ORO   R   OR   R   OR   OR
        | | | ∕∖   ∧ | ∕∖   ∧ | | ∧
      c om + i̯endo   cr e + i̯endo → cr e + žendo
                              ↓ (3.36)
                              ž

As shown, (3.36) applies only to *cre[i̯]endo,* where the [i̯] is syllable-initial. Syllable structure rules automatically "promote" the resulting [ž] to onset status, since this segment cannot be the first member of a rhyme.

In other cases the exact manner of operation of (3.36) is not so clear at first glance. Consider plural nouns like those illustrated in (3.32). It is not obvious how stem-final [i̯] comes to be syllable-initial, so that it meets the structural description of (3.36) and is thereby changed to [ž]. How this question arises is illustrated in the partial derivation given as (3.38):

(3.38) *Inner cycle:*

$$[[lei̯]_N \; es]_N \rightarrow [[\; l \; ei̯]_N \; es]_N$$
$$\qquad\qquad\qquad\qquad | \bigvee$$
$$\qquad\qquad\qquad\qquad OR$$

   Outer cycle:

In the inner cycle, syllable structure is assigned in the obvious and only possible way. But what is the result, in the outer cycle, of incorporating the newly available segments into prosodic structure? As we have developed them so far, the syllable structure rules of Spanish allow both the (a) and the (b) syllabifications. However, only in the (b) structure is

the glide [i̯] in syllable-initial position where it can be changed to [ž] by
rule (3.36), as desired. Must we add some new statement to the grammar of Spanish in order to guarantee this result?

It can be argued that this is unnecessary. Stated informally, the basis
for such an argument is the presumably uncontroversial proposition
that the syllabification V-CV is unmarked with respect to VC-V. Taking
V = [+syllabic] and C = [−syllabic], then (3.38b), the syllabification
required by the proposed grammar of Porteño, is unmarked with respect to (3.38a). Thus, (3.38b) should be preferred over (3.38a) in the
absence of a language-particular stipulation to the contrary.

Kiparsky's (1979) theory of syllable structure provides an elegant
formalization of the markedness proposition just enunciated. To see
this, consider the following elaborations of the representations of the
alternative outputs shown in (3.38a,b):

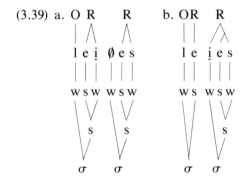

The structures shown *above* the segmental representations in (3.39) are
of course those of (3.38a,b), which the syllable structure rules of
Spanish might assign in the absence of any relevant general principles.
The binary trees, labeled according to the strong/weak relation, drawn
below the segmental representations are the structures relevant to
Kiparsky's theory. His "simplicity" condition (1979, 432–435), which
counts branches in such trees, designates (3.39b) as unmarked with respect to (3.39a), since (3.39b) has five branches whereas (3.39a) has six.
Marked structures can be assigned only at the cost of a language-
particular rule that overrides the provisos of the general theory.

In sum, (3.38b) (= (3.39b)) is selected cost free as the correct result
of cyclic syllable structure adjustment, simply and precisely by the *absence* of any contrary stipulation in the grammar of Spanish.[12]

Incidentally, I know of (only) one word that is apparently marked in Porteño in the sense of Kiparsky's "simplicity" condition. This word is *paranó*[i]*a,* whose syllabification is evidently (3.40a), in contrast with the syllabification of *argó*[ž]*a, cebó*[ž]*a, crió*[ž]*a, jó*[ž]*a, ó*[ž]*a, só*[ž]*a, tramó*[ž]*a,* etc., shown in (3.40b).

(3.40) a. paranóia   b. argó[ž]a

We must assume that the markedness principle in question is blocked by the lexical entry of *paranóia,* which is, in relevant respects, (3.40a). Lexical marking of the rhyme structure in the indicated substring prevents assignment of syllable structure according to the unmarked pattern, as discussed above for *leyes, creyendo,* etc.

I will now rectify some incorrect data given in Harris (1969, 33–36) which (along with neglect of syllable structure) led to a descriptive error. I was under the misapprehension that phrases like *hay una* 'there is one' and *(la) ley es* '(the) law is' could be pronounced [ažuna] and [ležes] in Porteño, segmentally identical to *ayuna* 'fast' and *leyes* 'laws', respectively. Not so: *ayuna* and *leyes* are indeed [ažuna] and [ležes], but *hay una* and *ley es* can be only [aiuna] and [leies].

We have seen how the phonetic representation of single words like *leyes* [ležes] is assigned. In the case of the many words like *ayuna* [ažuna], there is little of interest to say. Here, the [ž] is internal to the stem rather than stem-final, and it participates in no alternations. I therefore take the ž to be underlying and assign the representations /ažuna/, *ayer* /ažer/, *yo* /žo/, etc. What remains to be discussed, then, is the derivation of phrases like *hay una, ley es,* etc. The relevant portion of the derivation of *ley es* is shown in (3.41):

(3.41) [lei]ₙ [es]ᵥ → [l ei]ₙ [es]ᵥ

                    OR   R

Nothing else of immediate interest happens. In particular, resyllabification does not occur over the two words, because (as illustrated in section 2.7) this process shifts only [+consonantal] segments. The last segment of *ley* (*hay, convoy,* etc.) is a glide and thus immune. As a consequence, rule (3.36) cannot apply.

Notice that the account just suggested depends crucially on the assumption that Kiparsky's theory of markedness, whose role in the derivation of single words like *leyes* has already been described, plays no role in the derivation of phrases like *ley es*. Why should this be so? I believe that an answer can be given roughly along the following lines, although much remains to be made precise. Markedness principles of the type given in Kiparsky (1979) exert their effect when prosodically isolated segments are incorporated into syllable structure, either "from scratch" as in the first step (inner cycle) of (3.38) or as additions to existing structure as in the second step (outer cycle) of (3.38). When no segments remain unattached to prosodic structure, however, these principles do not have the "power" to alter structure already assigned by language-particular rules. The latter situation is illustrated in (3.41), in contrast to (3.38). If this answer is essentially correct, then Resyllabification (2.55) must be a rule of Spanish (as we had assumed), unlike the principle of markedness that governs word-internal syllable structure adjustment in cases like (3.38).

3.5 Types of *r*

3.5.1 The Basic Contrast

There is an astonishing variety of *r*-quality phones in Spanish. A phonetics teacher from whom I took undergraduate courses in Mexico claimed to have identified over 40 types of *r* in the Valley of Mexico alone. Fascinating though this fact is, it leaves open the question of how the phonological system of Spanish works. All investigators agree on at least this much: there is only one significant contrast, namely, the one illustrated in *foro* = *fo*[r]*o* 'forum' versus *forro* = *fo*[r̄]*o* 'lining' and many similar pairs. Between vowels, [r] contrasts with [r̄]. Both segments are syllable-initial in the examples cited. This contrast occurs only between vowels. In all other environments there is either free variation between [r] and [r̄] or obligatory neutralization in favor of one phone or set of phones. I thus reduce the vocabulary of symbols to just two, [r] and [r̄], which will be understood to jointly exhaust the rich phonetic variety mentioned at the beginning of this paragraph.

The standard realization of [r] is a single voiced alveolar flap, while [r̄] is articulated as a voiced alveolar trill of from two to ten or more extremely rapid vibrations. Of course, these are only the prototypical realizations. I will say little more about phonetic detail, since such information is readily available elsewhere (see, for example, Navarro

Tomás (1965)). Suffice it to say at this point that [r] and [r̄] are not "additive." By this I mean that clusters of these segments do not produce distinctively longer series of vibrations. For example:

(3.42) a. 'I left rapidly' ≠ 'to leave rapidly'
       salí rápido ≠ salir rápido
       /salí # rápido/ ≠ /salír # rápido/
       sal[ír̄]ápido = sal[ír̄]ápido
    b. 'strange shrimp' ≠ 'strange amber'
       gamba rara ≠ ámbar raro
       /gámba # rára/ ≠ ámbar # ráro/
       gamb[ar̄]ara = ámb[ar̄]aro

As shown, [r̄] alone is not distinct from [rr̄], unless, obviously, the two segments are deliberately separated by an artificial pause or naturally fall into separate phonological phrases. I believe that this is true for all dialects, whatever the range of possible realizations of [r] and [r̄] individually may be.[13] I record this fact as follows:

(3.43) [rr̄] is not distinct from [r̄].

Let us assume that rule (3.44) expresses exactly the content of (3.43):

(3.44) r → $\emptyset$ / ___ r̄

3.5.2 Onsets
Only the flap [r] occurs as the second member of two-segment onsets: p[r]ado, b[r]ravo, f[r]asco, t[r]apo, d[r]ama, c[r]áter, g[r]ato, etc.[14]

In syllable-initial position after a (necessarily heterosyllabic) consonant, [r̄] occurs to the exclusion of [r], e.g., hon-[r̄]a, al-[r̄]ededor, Is-[r̄]ael, etc., not *hon-[r]a, *al-[r]ededor, *Is-[r]ael. In Harris (1969, 52) I characterized by means of segmental features, independently of syllable structure, the set of consonants {p t k b d g f} after which [r] occurs, as opposed to the set {n l s} after which [r̄] occurs, and I formulated a rule that changes [r] to [r̄] in the environment following the feature complex defining the latter set of segments. Although this works technically, it is a descriptive mistake because it duplicates the work of syllable structure generalizations. The following formulations avoid this defect:

(3.45) r → r̄ / [+cons] ___   or   r → r̄ / [+cons] $_\sigma$[___

R

(The two formulations shown seem to have the same empirical content. A richer theory of rules with prosodic conditioning than is now available, however, may dictate a preference for one over the other.)

One property of rule (3.45) deserves comment: it is not immediately obvious that it relates any alternating forms. Rather, it seems to state a "static" positional constraint that holds inside morphemes. In other words, it is not clear that there are any morphemes with [r] in some environment alternating with [r̄] in another environment in accordance with rule (3.45). One candidate that is at least initially plausible is *honra* = *hon*-[r̄]*a* 'honor' and (only) partially synonymous *honor* = *hono*[r]. However, the synchronic relatedness of these two words is not self-evident. Their lack of total synonymy, different derivational possibilities,[15] and different terminal elements (-*a* in *honra* versus ∅ in *honor*) show, at the very least, that we are not dealing simply with an optional deletion of the second *o* of *honor* which would place the *r* in the domain of rule (3.45).

In word-initial position [r̄] occurs to the absolute exclusion of [r]; e.g., [r̄]*ata,* [r̄]*eto,* [r̄]*ito,* [r̄]*oto,* [r̄]*uta.* "Word-initial" must be taken literally here, as distinct from "utterance-initial." That is, [r̄] obligatorily excludes [r] at the beginning of a syntactic word regardless of its position in the phonological phrase: (pause)-[r̄]*ata, la* [r̄]*ata,* and under no circumstances **la* [r]*ata.*[16] Thus, the grammar of Spanish must have some device to obligatorily neutralize the [r]/[r̄] contrast in favor of [r̄] in word-initial position. I state this as (3.46),

(3.46)   r → r̄ / X^0[_____

where X^0 is understood to vary over all word-level syntactic category labels.

The question now arises with regard to rule (3.46)—as it did with rule (3.45)—whether the generalization expressed is an alternation or a "static" positional restriction. Examples like the following are suggestive:

(3.47) #[r̄]ec + titud *vs.* #e + [r]ec + ción   'uprightness'   'erection'

      #[r̄]up + tura   #e + [r]up + ción   'rupture'   'eruption'

      #[r̄]ub + or   #e + [r]ub + escente   'blush'   'blushing'

      #[r̄]o + er   #e + [r]o + sión   'to eat away'[17]   'erosion'

      #[r̄]ud + o   #e + [r]ud + ición   'stupid'   'erudition'

What (3.47) suggests is that rule (3.46) accounts for an alternation in morphemes like *rec-, rup-, rub-,* and so on, whose first segment appears as [r̄] in word-initial position but as [r] word-internally, in particular after the prefix *e-*. The trouble with these examples—the best I can find—is that the synchronic relatedness of certain pairs is less than obvious. In any event, the basic generalization behind rule (3.46) is clearly genuine—indeed exceptionless—at least as a positional constraint if not also as an alternation.[18]

3.5.3 Rhymes

The realization of *r*-type segments is highly variable in rhymes—noncontrastively, of course—in most or all dialects.[19] From this variability, however, we may extract a very simple basic generalization: [r] in casual speech alternates with [r̄] in highly emphatic speech if this segment is followed by a consonant or is utterance-final, that is, if it is in a rhyme. For example:

(3.48)   *Casual*   *Highly emphatic*
    martes: ma[r]tes ~ ma[r̄]tes   'Tuesday'
    mar: ma[r]   ~ ma[r̄]   'sea'

I thus propose the following rule:

(3.49) r → r̄   (in emphatic speech)
        |
        R

Note that this formulation correctly includes the case in which *r* is a rhyme element but does not occur in syllable-final position:

(3.50) supers-tición

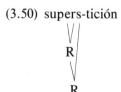

Words like *superstición* illustrate another important point. Suppose that we considered the representation *supe*[r̄]*s-tición* to reflect gemination of [r] rather than substitution of a distinct unitary phone. The second syllable would then be *perrs-*, with an otherwise unattested four-segment rhyme in internal position. This is obviously a bizarre and undesirable result.

Consider again in this connection words like *ropa* = [r̄]*opa, Enrique* = *En*[r̄]*ique*, in which *r* is obligatorily [r̄] in all styles of speech. Suppose again that [r̄] is equivalent to geminate [rr]. We would then have [rr]*opa, En*[rr]*ique*, and so on. How might such representations be syllabified? Not [r-r]*opa*, obviously, and not *En*[r-r]*ique* either, since *nr* is not a possible cluster in rhymes. Also not [rr]*o-pa, En-*[rr]*ique*, since *rr* violates all of the onset filters discussed in section 2.4. On the other hand, [r̄]*o-pa, En-*[r̄]*ique*, with [r̄] interpreted as a unitary segment, is a perfectly viable syllabification.

In short, it seems impossible to equate [r̄] with [rr]. Why would this equivalence come to mind in the first place? There are several reasons. Among others, we might take a hint from the (generally excellent) orthography, which represents [r]/[r̄] as *r/rr* in the contrastive intervocalic position; we might be influenced by the fact that for [r] the articulatory gesture is typically a single alveolar flap and for [r̄], two or more alveolar flaps. I will give other reasons later, but the fact remains: [r̄] is a single phonetic segment.

Returning now to rule (3.49), note that the directionality of this process has not been motivated. Why not (3.51) instead?

(3.51) r̄ → r
        |
        R

Consider cases like the following, of which there are many:

(3.52) a. *Inflection:* amo[r~r̄] / amo[r]es   'love' singular/plural
       b. *Derivation:*   amo[r]oso 'loving, affectionate'
                                       amo[r]ío   'love affair'

No case exists like *amo*[r~r̄]/**amo*[r̄]*es*, **amo*[r̄]*oso*, **amo*[r̄]*ío*, in which variable [r~r̄] in a rhyme alternates with [r̄] when the addition of an inflectional or derivational suffix places this segment in a syllable onset. Since syllable-initial intervocalic position is the environment in which [r] and [r̄] contrast, the phoneme of *amor̲es, amor̲oso*, etc., must be /r/ rather than /r̄/. Thus, *amo*[r~r̄] must be /amor/, and the directionality *r* → *r̄* rather than *r̄* → *r* in the optional rule (3.49) is established. This argument assumes, of course, that /r/ itself is not derived from some more basic segment, a traditional and apparently safe assumption.

3.5.4 The Contrast [r] and [r̄] between Vowels

Uncontroversially [r] is a single segment, and I have argued that [r̄] is also. Notoriously these segments contrast in intervocalic position, where both are syllable-initial. Minimal pairs are numerous indeed. For example:

(3.53)	to-[r]e-[r]o	*vs.*	to-[r̄]e-[r]o	'bullfighter'	'lighthouse keeper'
	que-[r]emos		que-[r̄]emos	'we want'	'we will want'
	ca-[r]o		ca-[r̄]o	'expensive'	'car'
	ce-[r]o		ce-[r̄]o	'zero'	'hill'
	pe-[r]a		pe[r̄]a	'pear'	'bitch'
	mi-[r]a		mi-[r̄]a	'gun sight'	'myrrh'

Is this contrast ultimately to be ascribed to two different phonemes /r/ and /r̄/? If not, what alternative can be motivated? Let us approach the matter obliquely.

We know that *r*, that is, [r], can occur in syllable-final position. Its occurrence in this environment is in fact quite unrestricted:

(3.54) *Before labials:* ar̲-pa, ár̲-b̲ol, gar̲-fio, ar̲-m̲a
      Before dentals: ar̲-t̲e, ar̲-d̲e, far̲-s̲a, sar̲-n̲a, Car̲-los
      Before palatal: mar̲-c̲ha
      Before velars: ar̲-c̲o, lar̲-g̲o, sar̲-gento = s̲a[r-x]e̲nto

We also know that *r*, that is, [r̄], occurs without restriction in syllable-initial position, as illustrated in (3.53) and elsewhere. It is therefore striking that we find exactly one gap in (3.54): [r-r]—and only [r-r]—is missing.[20]

Suppose that we want to account explicitly for this gap. This will require an ad hoc addition to the grammar, against the universal judgment that ad hoc additions are to be avoided whenever possible. We could avoid this one by simply dropping it, allowing heterosyllabic /r-r/ to occur in underlying representations and thus filling the gap in (3.54). We can—in fact do—then naturally take /r-r/ to be the source of [r̄] between vowels in phonetic representations. However, we know that [r̄] is a single segment. What cost is incurred by relating [r̄] to /r-r/? The answer is: none. The following derivation shows why.

(3.55) O R O R

| ∧ | | Syllable structure assignment
p e r r a   (uniquely determined)

r̄   Rule (3.45)

φ   Rule (3.44) (= (3.43))

pe-[r̄]*a*   Output

In short, simply doing nothing to an independently motivated grammar results in the correct phonetic output.[21] A very powerful argument— one which I see no reason to suppose can be constructed—is therefore necessary to justify any other move. I thus conclude that Spanish has a single *r* phoneme and that intervocalic [r̄] in phonetic representations derives from a (heterosyllabic) geminate cluster of this phoneme.

The conclusion just reached has some attractive consequences in three unexpected areas. Consider first the following forms, which illustrate a dependency between *r*-type segments and stress placement:

(3.56) *Penultimate stress*   *Antepenultimate stress*
[r]   [r̄]   [r]   *[r̄]
avá[r]a   chamá[r̄]a   cáma[r]a   *cáma[r̄]a
señó[r]a   camó[r̄]a   víbo[r]a   *víbo[r̄]a

As (3.56) suggests, there are no words with antepenultimate stress whose last syllable begins with [r̄]. More importantly, the absence of such words is not accidental: native speakers consistently judge nonce forms of this type to be deviant.[22] This situation would be a mystery if intervocalic [r̄] derived from a phoneme /r̄/ or any other single underlying segment. On the other hand, the data of (3.56) are explained, in the strong sense, if intervocalic [r̄] is derived from underlying heterosyllabic geminate *r:*

(3.57) cam ar-ra

R O

This is because antepenultimate stress is systematically impossible in words whose penultimate syllable has a branching rhyme, as was illustrated in the "second argument" of section 1.1.

 A second bonus can now be seen in the examples already given in (3.52). A wealth of examples in (2.45) illustrated that nouns and adjectives whose derivational stem ends in a cluster of [−syllabic] segments are always followed by one of the terminal elements -*o, -a, -e*. This provides the basis of an explanation, again in the strong sense, for the absence of alternations like *amo*[r]/**amo*[r̄]*es, amo*[r]/**amo*[r̄]*oso:* a stem such as *amorr-* requires a terminal element in order to be a word; therefore, *amorr-*, required for the inflected and derived forms, could not be the stem of the word *amor*. On the other hand, the data of (3.52) would be a mystery on the assumption of a single-segment source— say, /r̄/—for intervocalic [r̄]. There would be no non−ad hoc basis for the absence of words like **amo*/r̄/.

Third, derivation of intervocalic [r̄] from an underlying geminate makes available a uniquely non−ad hoc account of the irregular future stem *que*[r̄]- of the verb whose infinitive is *querer* 'to want'. Details aside, future tense verb forms in Spanish are constructed as illustrated in (3.58):

(3.58)   *Stem   Person−number endings*

    a. *Regular:*   comer-⎫

                 mover-⎬ -é, -ás, -á, etc.

    b. *Irregular:* podȩr-⎪

                 querȩr-⎭

As shown, a common set of person−number endings attaches to regular and irregular future stems alike. Regular stems are always identical to the infinitive. Thus, the future forms corresponding to the infinitive *comer* 'to eat' are regular *comeré, comerás*, etc. Irregular stems undergo deletion of the last vowel (and other modifications in more complex cases). Thus, the future forms corresponding to *poder* 'to be able' are irregular *podȩré → podré, podȩrás → podrás*, etc. Our proposal of a geminate source for intervocalic [r̄] makes possible exactly the same account for the irregular future forms of *querer: querȩré → que*[r̄]*é, querȩrás → que*[r̄]*ás*, etc. To derive [r̄] from any other source—say, /r̄/—requires either an otherwise unattested and unmotivated phonemic substitution, or suppletion.

In summary, the essential ingredients of the proposals made here concerning the distribution of [r] and [r̄] are brought together and displayed in (3.59):

(3.59) a. *Phonemic inventory:* one rhotic /r/
   b. *Rules:*
      (i) Syllable structure assignment (independently given)
      (ii) r → r̄ / [+cons] ____   (3.45)
            |
            R
      (iii) r → r̄ / $_{X^0}$[____   (3.46)
      (iv) r → ∅ / ____ r̄   (3.44 (= (3.43))
      (v) r → r̄   (in emphatic speech)   (3.49)
          |
          R

We have seen that the analysis summarized in (3.59) is strongly motivated on strictly distributional grounds and that it has advantageous
consequences for collateral areas of prosody and morphology. In short,
(3.59) enjoys a high degree of descriptive adequacy. I will not belabor
the point, but it will be obvious to those familiar with the treatment of
r-type phones in Harris (1969, 48–55) that the present account is much
better than the older one and that the improvement is due primarily to
the fact that attention is paid here to syllable structure.[23]
   To round out this section I will consider some additional data that
involve the interaction of optional rule (3.49) (= 3.59bv)) and the process of resyllabification. For convenience I will first repeat the basic
data that originally motivated rule (3.49).

(3.60) (=(3.48))   *Casual*   *Highly emphatic*
         martes: ma[r]tes ~ ma[r̄]tes   'Tuesday'
         mar: ma[r]   ~ ma[r̄]   'sea'

Now consider what happens when *r* in a rhyme is followed by another
word:

(3.61) *Alternation possible*   *Alternation impossible*
      mar verde: ma[r~r̄] verde   *mar azul:* ma[r, *r̄] azul
      'green sea'   'blue sea'

Word-final [r] alternates with [r̄] in emphatic speech if the next word
begins with a consonant but not if it begins with a vowel. If we take
syllable structure into account, especially as it is affected by the rule of
Resyllabification, we can find the crucial generalization in (3.60) and
(3.61). This is demonstrated in (3.62):

(3.62) mar # azul → ma r # azul ↛ *ma[ř] # azul

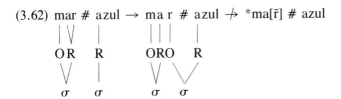

The initial representation of (3.62) shows the syllable structure of the individual words *mar, azul*. The second representation shows the result of Resyllabification; in particular, the final *r* of *mar* becomes an onset. Therefore, rule (3.49) cannot apply. This is the result that we want. In order for it to be available, however, we must be able to guarantee that (3.49) does not apply to the initial representation of (3.62), which would permit the ill-formed result shown in (3.63):

(3.63) mar # azul ──ᵃ──→ ma[ř] # azul ──ᵇ──→ *ma[ř] # azul[24]

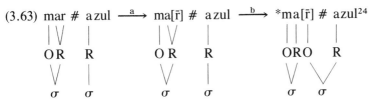

Step (a) indicates the operation of rule (3.49) and (b) the application of Resyllabification. What we must do is prevent (3.49) from applying before Resyllabification. In the next section I will sketch a general phonological theory that accommodates this restriction in a motivated and natural way.

3.6 Cyclic and Noncyclic Rules

Our task here will be to examine the relevance of the Spanish material studied above to two theories of the phonological cycle. The first is the theory of Mascaró (1976); the second is the one that is beginning to take shape in current investigation, which I will call *Lexical Phonology*.

In section 3.3 I argued that:

(a) A certain morphological constituent labeled [...]$_X$, where X = N, A, V, constitutes a cyclic domain for phonological rules. In verbs, [...]$_X$ contains the "derivational stem" (bracketed $(...)_x$) plus all inflectional morphemes. Nouns and adjectives, on the other hand, have the structure $[(...)_x ...]_X$ in the singular and $[[(...)_x ...]_X ...]_X$ in the plural. Adverbs, which are not inflected, are $[(...)_x ...]_X$. There is of course further structure internal to $(...)_x$, in all categories, in the case of derived words.

(b) Lateral Depalatalization (3.15) and Nasal Depalatalization (3.22) apply cyclically, in the domain $[...]_x$.

(c) Syllable structure assignment is also cyclic and also applies in the domain $[...]_x$.

These are hardly revolutionary proposals. The idea of cyclic rule application can be traced back, in the literature most readers are familiar with, at least to Chomsky, Halle, and Lukoff (1956). For Spanish, cyclic rules are proposed in Brame (1974) and Harris (1969, 1974). To be sure, these are stress rules, unlike the segmental rules of Lateral and Nasal Depalatalization. In the latter works it was taken for granted that the burden of proof fell on the proponent of a cyclic analysis. This position was based on the widely held belief, which I shared, that cyclic rules entail an undesirable loosening of phonological theory and that noncyclic rules therefore represent the null hypothesis. However, this belief is mistaken. We owe to Mascaró (1976) the argument that the admission of cyclic phonological rules indeed changes the class of possible grammars, but does not necessarily enlarge it. A cyclic theory of phonology is not automatically less constrained than a noncyclic theory. In short, there is no known a priori or methodological argument against cyclic phonological rules. Whether and which phonological rules are cyclic is a purely empirical question.

We also owe to Mascaró (1976) a highly articulated theory of cyclicity in phonology. Mascaró studied 22 phonological rules of Catalan, of which he argues 14 to be obligatory neutralization rules. He argues further that each of these 14 rules applies only in derived contexts (that is, internal to a morpheme if a crucial part of the context triggering the rule is itself derived by an earlier rule or across a morpheme boundary). This leads him to a precise and interesting formulation of the principle of (phonological) *Strict Cyclicity*. This principle can be stated roughly (but adequately for present purposes) as (3.64):

(3.64) Obligatory neutralization rules apply
    a. only in derived contexts   ("strict")
    b. cyclically   ("cyclicity")

Let us examine the Spanish rules of Lateral and Nasal Depalatalization with reference to (3.64). I have argued above that these rules are cyclic (3.64b). Are their other properties consistent with (3.64)? It is easy to determine that they are. First, it is obvious that both rules are categorically obligatory. Forms such as those in (3.65) cannot and do not ever arise through optional nonapplication of these rules:

(3.65) *belldad *reñcilla
       *éll   *desdéñ

It is equally obvious that both rules are neutralizing in the relevant sense, since both nonpalatal *l* and nonpalatal *n* are underlying segments—in fact very common ones—in Spanish, a fact that hardly needs documentation. The remaining question then is whether Lateral and Nasal Depalatalization can apply in nonderived contexts. It is clear from the form of the rules (3.15) and (3.22) themselves that they cannot, since the environment of both rules makes crucial use of information supplied by syllable structure rules. This was illustrated in (3.19) and (3.26), where, it will be recalled, in each derivation the depalatalization rule applies as the second step since it is (intrinsically) fed by syllable structure assignment as a first step, which creates a derived environment.[25] In short, Nasal Depalatalization (3.22) and Lateral Depalatalization (3.15) are consistent with the principle of Strict Cyclicity in phonology (3.64), whose empirical support is thereby broadened.

What is the status of the rules of syllable structure assignment in this respect? On the one hand, they feed other rules that apply in the first cycle, as we have seen. On the other hand, there is no known evidence that syllable structure rules are themselves fed by anything. Yet it is unacceptable to represent directly in the lexicon the syllable structure of underived representations, even if it could technically be done. This follows from the fact that syllable structure in underived contexts is just as predictable as in derived contexts, and furthermore obeys exactly the same generalizations. Moreover, evidence has been presented above that the rules of syllable structure assignment do in fact apply cyclically. But syllable structure rules are patently not neutralization rules, under any intelligible interpretation of "neutralization." In short, syllable structure rules are not consistent with (3.64): they are cyclic, but not strict cyclic, and they are not neutralizing.

Consider again the rule of Aspiration (3.3b) discussed in section 3.1, which changes *s* to [h] under certain conditions. We will be concerned now with only those aspects of the rule that are relevant to its status as cyclic or noncyclic. First, it can hardly be doubted that Aspiration is neutralizing in some dialects. Specifically, there are known to be dialects that have /h/ in their inventory of underlying phonemes and also make use of Aspiration, whose output is [h]. (The most accessible reference on this point for many readers may be Canfield (1962, 73–74, 81–82, maps III and IV).)

Next, I will argue that Aspiration is not a cyclic rule. I will use a reductio ad absurdum argument; that is, I will demonstrate that cyclic application of this rule inevitably produces incorrect results. Consider the derivation of *meses* 'months' (singular *mes*) given in (3.66):

(3.66) *Inner cycle:*

$$[[mes]_N \ es]_N \xrightarrow{\ a\ } [[mes]_N \ es]_N \xrightarrow{\ b\ } [[meh]_N \ es]_N$$

$$\qquad\quad \text{R} \qquad\qquad\qquad \text{R}$$

Outer cycle:

$$[\ meh \ es]_N \xrightarrow{\ a\ } [\ me h \ es]_N \xrightarrow{\ b\ } *[\ me h \ eh]_N$$

$$\qquad \text{R} \qquad\qquad\quad \text{O R} \qquad\qquad\quad \text{O R}$$

In both cycles, step (a) is of course syllable structure (re)assignment and step (b) is Aspiration. The output of the first cycle, *me*[h], is in fact the correct representation of the singular. However, this representation is inexorably carried into the second cycle to ultimately give the incorrect plural representation **me*[h]*e*[h] instead of correct *me*[s]*e*[h]. Clearly, the internal *s* of *meses* (and all analogous cases) must never undergo Aspiration; equally clearly, this correct result can be produced only if Aspiration does not apply cyclically.[26]

Note that the desired exclusion of Aspiration from the first cycle cannot be achieved by appeal to the "strict" clause (3.64a) of the Strict Cyclicity principle. This is because Aspiration is crucially dependent on and fed by syllable structure assignment.

The remaining question is whether or not Aspiration is obligatory. This question is crucial because a clear and interesting empirical prediction depends on the answer. The Strict Cyclicity principle (3.64) requires that if Aspiration is or becomes obligatory in some dialect in which it is also neutralizing, then it must concomitantly be or become cyclic. A specific consequence is that the plural of words like *mes* must change immediately from *me*[s]*e*[h] to *me*[h]*e*[h] in a dialect in which Aspiration becomes obligatory (in addition to being neutralizing).

The facts are as follows. Uncontroversially, Aspiration is optional in many dialects. Indeed, it is the study of the precise nature of the variability of this rule that has occupied so many investigators and led to the accumulation of a vast literature. On the other hand, it seems a virtual certainty that Aspiration has become an obligatory rule for some speakers.[27] Yet no investigator has ever reported that any speaker has ever uttered the pronunciations, say, *me[h]e[h], *ve[h]e[h], *to[h]e[h], *vo[h]e[h], etc., rather than me[s]e[h], ve[s]e[h], to[s]e[h], vo[s]e[h], etc., as the plurals of words like mes 'month', vez 'time', tos 'cough', voz 'voice', etc., which are so common that they could hardly escape notice.

We are thus led to conclude that the Strict Cyclicity principle (3.64)—or rather the more careful formulation of Mascaró (1976)—does not correctly characterize the class of cyclic phonological rules. We have seen that syllable structure rules falsify (3.64) in one direction: they are cyclic and obligatory, but not neutralizing. The rule of Aspiration, on the other hand, evidently falsifies the Strict Cyclicity principle in another direction: it is (presumably for some speakers) obligatory and neutralizing, but not cyclic.

The theory of the cycle in phonology has been further elucidated since Mascaró (1976), notably in Kiparsky (1979), Halle (1980), Pesetsky (1979), Rubach (1980, forthcoming), Mohanan (1981, 1982), among other current studies. The picture that is emerging from the most recent investigations can be visualized roughly as follows:

(3.67)

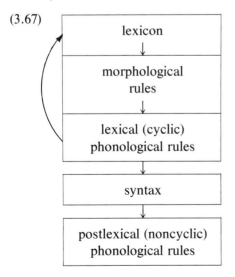

The theory suggested by the flowchart in (3.67) has been dubbed *Lexical Phonology* because it postulates a set of phonological rules that apply within the lexicon. That is, as (3.67) indicates, the output of one (lexical) phonological cycle is a potential input to another round of application of morphological and phonological rules. When all such lexical processes are exhausted, the output is available for insertion into a syntactic structure. Finally, a set of postlexical phonological rules applies to word-sized or larger units.

It is not my aim here to give a detailed exposition of Lexical Phonology, which is still in the early stages of development and evolving rapidly, or to review systematically the evidence that has been adduced in its favor. It is also not my goal to produce a partisan manifesto for Lexical Phonology on the basis of the Spanish material examined above. Rather, having seen that this material presents serious difficulties for the most highly articulated theory of the phonological cycle available to date, namely, Mascaró (1976), I will consider briefly how well the emerging theory of Lexical Phonology fares vis-à-vis the description of Spanish presented here. Anticipating a bit, Lexical Phonology fares quite well: it seems to be inconsistent with none of the results I have established, while actually predicting some of them.

At the start of this section I reviewed the claim made in section 3.3 regarding the domain of cyclicity of syllable structure rules and Lateral and Nasal Depalatalization, namely, $[...]_X$, where $X = N, A, V$. Under familiar "lexicalist" syntactic assumptions prevalent since Chomsky (1970), this result is in fact predicted by the version of Lexical Phonology depicted in (3.67). That is, the organization of (3.67) requires that the level of lexical insertion into syntactic structure (X^0 in an X-bar system) coincide with a cyclic domain. The grammar of Spanish thus needs no language-particular stipulation to this effect.[28]

As noted earlier, syllabic structure rules violate the principle of Strict Cyclicity in that they must apply in nonderived as well as derived contexts. One characteristic of these rules that clearly sets them apart from garden-variety phonological rules is that syllable structure rules do not change features. Rather, they belong to the class of rules that *assign* features and/or prosodic structure that is lexically *unspecified*. Although not shown in (3.67), it is one of the central tenets of Lexical Phonology that rules which assign lexically unspecified features/ structures apply within the lexicon. Thus, the (empirically correct) stipulation that syllable structure assignment rules are cyclic can be transferred from the grammar of Spanish to the general theory.[29]

Recall now the rule of Resyllabification (2.55). Unlike the (lexical) rules of syllable structure assignment, this rule has as its sole function that of adjusting already assigned structure, at the juncture of two syntactic words. There is no evidence that Resyllabification must apply cyclically. Therefore, in terms of (3.67), Resyllabification is a postlexical rule, and its properties are fully consistent with Lexical Phonology.

Next, let us consider the interaction of Resyllabification with other rules. Section 3.5 demonstrates that the emphatic-speech rule of "*r*-Strengthening" (3.49) (= (3.59bv)), which changes [r] to [r̄] in rhymes, must apply *after* Resyllabification. Specifically, (3.62) illustrates that correct outputs (e.g., (3.68a)) result from the order (Resyllabification, *r*-Strengthening) and (3.63) that incorrect outputs (e.g., (3.68b)) are produced by the opposite order.

(3.68) a. ma[r] # azul   b. *ma[r̄] # [azul]

    O   R   O   R

In terms of (3.67), optional *r*-Strengthening is a postlexical rule, and its properties are consistent with Lexical Phonology. Given that *r*-Strengthening is postlexical, its order with respect to (postlexical) Resyllabification is predictable on the not implausible assumption that prosodic rules precede segmental rules of the same (lexical or postlexical) type, at least in the unmarked case.

At this point a potential misunderstanding should be averted. It is not the case that postlexical rules apply only at boundaries within a phrase. Rather, they apply wherever their structural description is met, within or at the edges of a constituent, but after the lexical cycle is exhausted. Thus, *r*-Strengthening can apply word-internally in (3.69a) just as it can in the phrase (3.69b).

(3.69) a. martes   'Tuesday'   (→ ma[r̄]tes)

    R

   b. mar # tranquilo 'calm sea'   (→ ma[r̄] tranquilo)

    R

Since it is postlexical, however, r-Strengthening cannot apply internally in the plural *mares* 'seas' (= [[mar]$_N$ es]$_N$) any more than it can in
the phrase *mar # azul* since the output of (lexical) syllable structure
rules is (3.70), where the [r] occurs in an onset.

(3.70) ma r es
        | | | \/
        ORO R

In the same vein, rule (3.43) (= (3.44), (3.59biv)), which establishes
that [r̄] and [rr̄] are nondistinct—and which we may call *Nondistinctness* for convenience—must be postlexical since it guarantees the phonetic equivalence of phrases like *salí* [r̄]*ápido* 'I left fast' and *salír*
[r̄]*ápido* 'to leave fast' as *sal*[ír̄á]*pido*. Given the considerations of the
previous paragraph, the fact that Nondistinctness is a postlexical rule
does not imply that it cannot apply word-internally after other lexical
or postlexical rules. In particular, there is no obstacle to derivations
like (3.71a,b):

(3.71) a. RO   b.   R   O
           /\| /\ |
         per r o   quer + r é   Syllable structure assignment

           r̄   r̄   Rule (3.45)

           Ø   Ø   Nondistinctness

         pe[r̄]o   que[r̄]é   Phonetic output

(Nondistinctness, by the way, is a noncyclic obligatory neutralization
rule, in defiance of the Strict Cyclicity principle.)

   To pursue a different line now, in the earlier discussion of Strict Cyclicity, derivation (3.66) illustrates that the rule of Aspiration, unlike
Lateral and Nasal Depalatalization, produces incorrect results if allowed to apply on word-internal cycles. The same is true of the rule of
Velarization (3.3a), discussed along with Aspiration in section 3.1,
which changes [n] to [ŋ] in rhymes.[30] This is illustrated in the derivation
of *trenes* 'trains' (singular *tren*) given in (3.72):

(3.72) *Inner cycle:*

   [[tren]$_N$ es]$_N$ $\xrightarrow{a}$ [[tren]$_N$ es]$_N$ $\xrightarrow{b}$ [[treŋ]$_N$ es]$_N$
            \/   \/
            R   R

Outer cycle:

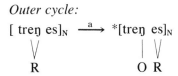

This derivation is analogous to that of *me*[h]*e*[h] in (3.66). Step (a) is syllable structure (re)assignment and step (b) is Velarization. The output of the first cycle, *tre*[ŋ], is the correct representation of the singular. But the output of the second cycle should be *tre*[n]*es* rather than **tre*[ŋ]*es*. It is obvious that this incorrect result can be avoided by prohibiting Velarization from applying in the first cycle.

Having established that Aspiration and Velarization must be prevented from applying in word-internal cycles, we now ask how these two rules interact with postlexical Resyllabification (2.55). An answer to this question is already in hand; indeed, it was one of the central concerns of section 3.1. The derivations given there in (3.5) show that Velarization and Aspiration must apply *before* Resyllabification in order to produce desired outputs like (3.73a,b):

(3.73) a. Ramó[ŋ] # entró   b. tiene[h] # espacio

We are thus led to this conclusion: Aspiration and Velarization must be prevented from applying in word-internal (lexical) cycles but they must apply before postlexical Resyllabification. How can this conclusion be made consistent with the organization of grammar displayed in (3.37), that of Lexical Phonology? (We do not wish to accept an answer that forces us to abandon the assumption that prosodic rules precede segmental rules of the same type—lexical or postlexical—in the unmarked case.) In familiar terminology, Aspiration and Velarization are "word-level" rules; that is, rules that apply exactly once, at the level of the lexical word. Evidently then, Lexical Phonology must allow for a partitioning of lexical rules into a (fully) cyclic set and a last-cyclic (= word-level) set. I will not pursue the formal characterization of this partitioning here. (Mohanan (1982) studies relevant issues in some detail.)

Not all of the rules mentioned in this study have been reexamined in the light of Lexical Phonology. We are in a position, however, to set out the following illustrative taxonomy of rules:[31]

(3.74)

A. Lexical
  (i) Prosodic
    Syllable structure assignment   (obligatory, nonneutralizing)
  (ii) Segmental
    a. "fully cyclic"
      Lateral Depalatalization   (obligatory, neutralizing)
      Nasal Depalatalization   (obligatory, neutralizing)
    b. "last cyclic"
      Aspiration   ($\pm$obligatory, $\pm$neutralizing)
      Velarization   ($\pm$obligatory, nonneutralizing)

B. Postlexical
  (i) Prosodic
    Resyllabification   (obligatory, ?neutralizing)
  (ii) Segmental
    r-Strengthening   (optional, nonneutralizing)
    Nondistinctness   (obligatory, neutralizing)

Neither Resyllabification nor *r*-Strengthening absolutely must apply to every representation that meets its structural description. Nevertheless, I have classified Resyllabification as obligatory and *r*-Strengthening as optional because the conditions for their application are different: the colloquial norm is application for Resyllabification but nonapplication for *r*-Strengthening. (I cannot decide whether it makes sense to classify Resyllabification as either neutralizing or nonneutralizing; nothing hinges on the decision.)

It is not clear how, or indeed whether, the status of a given rule as lexical or postlexical (and if lexical, as fully or last cyclic) can be predicted. (What does seem to be clear is that obligatory versus optional and neutralizing versus nonneutralizing are not the relevant criteria.) This question will be left as a challenge for future research. I will observe in closing, however, that at least for Spanish it is not necessary to search far and wide for crucial examples. Quite the contrary: relevant examples are extremely common, in the ordinary inflections of everyday nouns, adjectives, and verbs. Thus, it is possible that the language learner (or the linguist) could hear sufficient evidence in any typical five-minute stretch of speech to determine empirically the status of any—in fact all—of the rules in question.

Part II

STRESS ASSIGNMENT
IN SPANISH

Chapter 4
Basic Data

4.1 Introduction

4.1.1 Theoretical Results
In order to account for contrasts in stress placement such as *sábana/ sabána/Panamá*, along with other facts about stress in Spanish, previous analyses have employed an array of lexical diacritics and other exception-marking devices. The present analysis dispenses with such machinery. All of the peculiarities of Spanish stress heretofore attributed to such devices are shown to follow from independently motivated morphological structures plus the contrast "marked vs. unmarked" stress placement. Markedness, in turn, is interpreted in terms of the universal theory of *extrametricality* (Hayes (1979, 1980)). I will formulate and illustrate the Peripherality Condition, a universal principle which both strongly constrains the theory of extrametricality and has highly desirable consequences in the grammar of Spanish. The results obtained here for Spanish allow us to contemplate an extremely restrictive phonological theory in which all language-particular lexical stress-marking diacritics are excluded.

4.1.2 Background
Liberman and Prince's important article on English stress (1977), along with other recent work on metrical or prosodic theory,[1] provides a powerful incentive to reexamine the stress sytems of well-studied languages. I have begun to do this for Spanish, and in the process have discovered some primary data whose significance has gone unrecognized in previous studies. In the following discussions I will incorporate this new material into an adequate description of Spanish word stress, and investigate the relevance of the revised description to issues that

arise in prosodic or metrical stress theories, especially the notion of extrametricality.

Generative phonologists have produced detailed accounts of Spanish word stress on a fairly frequent schedule. (For example, in chronological order, Foley (1965), Harris (1969, 1975), Hooper and Terrell (1976), Whitley (1976), Contreras (1977), Solan (1979), among others.) In this literature there are of course differences in style of argumentation, variations in emphasis on one or another aspect of the data, and incompatible theoretical biases and claims. Nonetheless, there are areas of agreement regarding data and description that are no less conspicuous and no less significant than the differences. In order to provide perspective for new arguments, I will outline now, with a minimum of exemplification and no explicit review of the literature, those aspects of Spanish word stress that I take to have been firmly established.

4.2 Established Generalizations

4.2.1 Morphological Government of Verb Stress
Segmental phonological representation and morphological identification are jointly necessary and sufficient to determine placement of word stress for all verb forms. Each inflectional paradigm and nonparadigmatic form (infinitive, gerund, participle) has a characteristic fixed stress pattern that admits no variation, however minimal, among individual lexical items. There is no such thing as an unpredictably or irregularly stressed verb form in Spanish. (This does not mean, of course, that the principles governing verb stress are fully understood; however, in what follows verbs are excluded from discussion unless explicitly mentioned.)

4.2.2 Lexical Government of Nonverb Stress
Segmental representation and morphological characterization are (necessary but) not sufficient to determine word stress in members of lexical categories other than verbs. For example, imagine that /atapama/ is the segmental representation of a noun. The stress of this hypothetical word is unpredictable: *atápama, atapáma,* and *atapamá* are all possible. Information must be supplied in the lexicon regarding the stress of individual items. The same is true of adjectives and adverbs.

4.2.3 Prosodic Restrictions
Although lexical information is necessary, stress placement is not totally free. Spanish retains the following residual effects of the Latin stress rule:

(a) Stress must fall on one of the last three syllables of the word. Although *atápama, atapáma* are well-formed hypothetical words, **átapama* is not.

(b) Antepenultimate stress is impossible if the permit is a closed syllable. Hypothetical *atapámba* and *atapambá* are well formed but **atápamba* is not (nor is **átapamba*, of course).

4.2.4 Markedness
Although stress may appear on any one of the last three syllables of a word (with the qualification just noted), not all possibilities are equally likely. A wide range of evidence has been brought forward that supports the following statements about markedness:

(a) *Penultimate stress is unmarked in vowel-final words.* Thus, we find unmarked *pistóla, perdída, sabána,* versus marked *epístola, pérdida, sábana.* The status of vowel-final oxytones, e.g., *paletó, Panamá,* is less obvious; they feel less natural than vowel-final paroxytones, but it has proven difficult to provide a satisfactory formalization compatible with the assumption that they are marked.

(b) *Final stress is unmarked in consonant-final words.* Thus, we have unmarked *civíl, mercéd, altár* versus marked *móvil, césped, ámbar.* Plurals of words like *sábana, móvil,* etc., have proparoxytone stress, as expected: *sábanas, móviles,* and so on. Otherwise, proparoxytone stress in consonant-final words is severely restricted. It occurs in only two sets of forms: (i) a sizable group of words of Greek origin like *síntesis, ósmosis, análisis, sífilis, isósceles, Sócrates,* etc., and (ii) a small group of random idiosyncratic words like *régimen, Júpiter, Álvarez,* and possibly two or three others, depending on the extent of one's erudition.

4.2.5 Nonprimary Stresses
Spanish has two patterns of word-internal nonprimary stresses:

(4.1) a. gèneratívo, gràmaticàlidád, Pànamá
      b. genèratívo, gramàticàlidád, àntigèr eràtivísta

Weaker-than-primary stresses—usually recorded in the literature as tertiary in the Trager–Smith notation—may appear (a) on the initial syllable, or (b) on even-numbered syllables counting leftward from the primary stress, subject to the condition that nonprimaries cannot occur adjacent to each other or to the primary (*grà̱màticàlidád, *bà̱ndáda).[2] The (a) pattern is colloquial; the (b) pattern has a rhetorical tinge and is often heard in newscasting, in lecturing, and in highlighted chunks of otherwise informal speech.[3]

4.3 Cyclic and Noncyclic Stress Assignment

A borderline section between "established generalizations" and "new data" is needed for this topic. Brame (1974) and Harris (1969, 1974) presented arguments that stress is assigned cyclically in two morphological classes of nonverb forms, namely, adverbs with the suffix -mente '-ly' and diminutives with the productive suffixes -ito and -(e)cito. In the studies just cited the claim is implicit that stress is noncyclic outside these sets of words. As mentioned in section 3.6, however, the point was not argued explicitly because most linguists took it for granted that noncyclicity was the null hypothesis, though it seems clear now that this view is incorrect. These historical details aside, there are prosodic contrasts in Spanish that provide the basis for an argument supporting not only the claim that stress assignment is cyclic in -mente adverbs and productively formed diminutives but also the claim that it is noncyclic in other cases. I turn to such data now.

Preservation of prominence relations under subordination is of course the primary characteristic of cyclicity in stress assignment. Bearing this in mind, consider the following examples. Observe the relationship of the stress pattern of the adjectives (4.2a) to that of the derived adverbs (4.2b) on the one hand, and to that of the other derived forms (4.2c) on the other hand.

(4.2) *Adjective stress:* *Final*   *Penultimate*   *Antepenultimate*
   a. *Adjective:*   fŏrmál   sĕncíllo   hĭstórĭcŏ
   b. *Adverb:*   fŏrmàlméntĕ   sĕncìllàméntĕ   hĭstòrĭcàméntĕ
   c. *Other:*   fòrmălísmŏ   sèncĭlléz   hìstŏrĭcĭdád

The adverb-forming suffix -mente attaches to adjectives; the stress contour of the adjective pronounced in isolation is retained in the adverb. The stress patterns of the words with "other" suffixes are those just shown in section 4.2.5, which depend only on the position of primary stress in the derived word. Crucially, these are identical to those found in words with no relevant internal structure, for example, relatively long toponyms like *Àcapúlco, Tègucigálpa,* or *Tegùcigálpa, Chìchicàstenángo, Tròmpipendécuaro,* and so on. It is obvious, then, that cyclic and noncyclic stress assignment to *-mente* adverbs and "other" forms, respectively, predicts exactly the contrast illustrated.

In the productive class of noun and adjective diminutives, the stress itself of inner constituents is not preserved under embedding, but stress-dependent phenomena—such as diphthongization—do persist. For example:

(4.3) *Underived*   *Diminutive* vs. *Other*
     fu̲érte 'strong'   fu̲èrtecíto   fòrtaléza 'strength, stronghold'
     vi̲éjo   'old'   vi̲ĕjíto   vĕjéte   'little old man'

In the diminutives, diphthongs continue to appear under weaker-than-primary stress, just as they do when they bear primary stress in underived words. In the "other" cases, however, the expected monophthongs appear under weaker-than-primary stress. This contrast is readily accounted for if stress is assigned cyclically and noncyclically, respectively, in the two cases. The diminutives involve one additional step, not found in *-mente* adverbs: nonrightmost primary stresses are eliminated; e.g., *fuértecíto → fuĕrtecíto, viéjíto → viĕjíto.* Consequently, minor stresses appear in the expected pattern; e.g., *fuèrtecíto* (cf. *fòrmalísmo, Àcapúlco*) and *viĕjíto* rather than **vièjíto* (cf. *băndáda, *bàndáda*).[4]

In the following discussion, I will concentrate first on the principles that determine relations of prominence in the noncyclic cases, a logical prerequisite to the study of the cyclic cases, to which I will finally return in section 5.3.2.

4.4 New Data

No description of Spanish stress that I am aware of gives an account of the material to be discussed in this section. Apparently, this is simply because the significance of these data has not been appreciated by investigators, including myself. Certainly the forms themselves are not obscure, nor are the judgments of well-formedness cloudy or dialectally limited.

4.4.1 Branching Penults

We have already seen that antepenultimate stress is not possible if the penult is closed (*atápamba*, etc.). The Latin stress rule has left the further residual effect that not only consonants but also glides may not close penults in proparoxytones: *atápa[i̯]ba*, *atápa[u̯]ba*, etc.[5] More interestingly, antepenultimate stress is also impossible if the penult contains a prevocalic glide: *atáp[i̯]aba*, *atáp[u̯]eba*, etc. The generalization that emerges is thus that antepenultimate stress is impossible if the penultimate syllable has a branching rhyme.[6] This generalization does not appear in any existing description for the simple reason that no existing description is formulated in terms of intrasyllabic constituents. It is also the case, so far as I can see, that this generalization cannot even be incorporated into available descriptions of Spanish except as an ad hoc accretion, for reasons that will become clearer as we proceed.

4.4.2 Glide-final Words

As observed in section 4.2.4, stress on a nonfinal syllable of a consonant-final word is possible but marked. A qualification is necessary: if the final "consonant" is a glide, nonfinal stress is impossible. More specifically, glide-final nonoxytones are not marked or accidentally missing; rather, they are totally unacceptable. For example, native speakers vigorously reject hypothetical forms such as *cónvoy, *mámey, *ábre[u̯]. On the other hand, glide-final oxytones (exist and) are well formed: convóy, caráy, maméy, Abré[u̯], Palá[u̯], Arrá[u̯], and so on. (I can find only proper nouns with final [u̯].) This difference between glides and other nonsyllabic segments is a mystery for all existing descriptions.

Suppose that we group glides not with consonants but instead with other nonconsonantal segments, i.e., vowels. The problem does not disappear: stress may fall on the third [−consonantal] segment from the right in vowel-final words (*sábana, epístola*, etc.) but not in glide-final words (*cónvoy*, etc.). This too is a mystery for all available descriptions.

4.4.3 Diphthongs in Final Syllables

We have just seen that word-final glides allow stress only on the final syllable. It is also the case that final syllables with prevocalic glides exclude antepenultimate stress. For example, the position of stress in (necessarily hypothetical) *atápam[i̯]a*, *atápam[u̯]a*, and so on, is judged by native speakers to be clearly unacceptable.

It is tempting to see this exclusion and the exclusion of stress four syllables back from the right end of the word (*átapama*) as precisely the same fact. If the prenuclear glide were a vowel, or counted the same as a vowel, then the two cases would be parallel:

(4.4) *atápami a

   | | | |

   *átapama

Furthermore, there is no surface contrast between glides and unstressed high vowels in the indicated position of atapam̱ia. We can thus envision derivations like the following:

(4.5) /atapamia/

    á   Stress assignment

    i̯   [V, −stress, +high] → G / ___ V

  [atapámi̯a] Surface representation

On this proposal, a form like *[atápami̯a] is impossible because stress cannot be placed farther to the left than in the sample derivation, that is, on the third nonconsonantal segment (glide or vowel) from the right edge of the word.

Attractive though this suggestion may seem, there are several reasons why it cannot help to explain the material under discussion. First, as pointed out earlier, it does not generalize to the case of glide-final words, which can be stressed only on the rightmost syllable. Graphically, there is no parallelism here:

(4.6) *atápamia *or* *atápami a *or* *atápami a

  | | || | | || | | ||

  *áta i̯   *át_ ai̯   *áta _i̯

Second, independently of glide-final words, it is impossible to maintain that stress cannot be placed on a glide or vowel farther to the left than the third one from the right edge of the word. This is shown by abundant and perfectly acceptable words like *náufrago, cáustico,*

                                          1 2 3 4   12 3 4

áureo, farmacéutico, etc., in which primary word stress obviously falls

 1 2 34   12 3 4

on the fourth nonconsonantal segment from the right end of the word.

The restriction under discussion is reminiscent of the generalization that emerged in section 4.4.1, namely, that proparoxytones do not have branching rhymes in the penultimate syllable. Could the full generalization be that proparoxytones also may not have branching rhymes in the final syllable? Apparently not, since there are three sources of proparoxytones with branching final rhymes:

(4.7) a. *Ordinary plurals:* sábana̱s̱, católico̱s̱, cadávere̱s̱, automóvile̱s̱, etc.
   b. *Greek singulars:* hipótesi̱s̱, parálisi̱s̱, etc.
   c. *Miscellaneous:* espécime̱ṉ, Álvare̱ẕ, etc.

The first group is of course very large, the second nonnegligible, and the third limited to a handful of words. I will later reassess the evidence that such examples provide. At the moment, however, they present a serious obstacle to the generalization that branching rhymes in either the penult or the final syllable of a word are incompatible with antepenultimate stress.

In short, we seem to be facing a new restriction—"Final syllables with prevocalic glides exclude antepenultimate stress"—that cannot be reduced to or formally associated with any other generalization. Not surprisingly, this restriction does not follow as a consequence from any existing description.[7]

Chapter 5
Prosodic Structures and Extrametricality

5.1 Setting the Stage: Morphological and Prosodic Structures

5.1.1 The Domain of Stress Assignment

I will argue in this section that the domain of stress assignment in Spanish is the "word"—defined here by $[\ldots]_X$ (where X = Noun, Adjective, or Adverb). When this is established, the contrast between cyclic and noncyclic application of stress rules illustrated in section 4.3 can be described in a principled way.

In the case of nouns, adjectives, and adverbs, Spanish "words" are composed of a "derivational stem" optionally followed by a "terminal element." In the following examples, words are enclosed in square brackets labeled with uppercase letters, and derivational stems are enclosed in parentheses labeled with lowercase letters.[1] I use A/a for both adjectives and adverbs since nothing in the immediate context hinges on the distinction.

(5.1)

Nouns	Adjectives	Adverbs
$[(sed)_n \ a]_N$	$[(alert)_a \ a]_A$	$[(cerc)_a \ a]_A$
$[(ded)_n \ o]_N$	$[(blanc)_a \ o]_A$	$[(dentr)_a \ o]_A$
$[(sed)_n \ e]_N$	$[(verd)_a \ e]_A$	$[(adelant)_a \ e]_A$
$[(sed)_n \ ]_N$	$[(azul)_a \ ]_A$	$[(atrás)_a \ ]_A$
$[(dos)_n \ is]_N$	$[(isóscel)_a \ es]_A$	$[(lej)_a \ os]_A$
'silk'	'alert'	'near'
'finger'	'white'	'inside'
'seat'	'green'	'ahead'
'thirst'	'blue'	'behind'
'dose'	'isosceles'	'far'

The derivational stem is so named because it is the constituent to which derivational morphemes are attached. For example:

(5.2) sediento   'thirsty' = [((sed)$_n$ ient)$_a$ o]$_A$
                  thirst-y   -TE
      blancura 'whiteness' = [((blanc)$_a$ ur)$_n$ a]$_N$
                  white -ness -TE
      verdoso   'greenish' = [((verd)$_a$ os)$_a$ o]$_A$
                  green -ish -TE

Note, crucially, that terminal elements appear only at the outermost layer of morphological structure, i.e., at the level of the word. Longer examples than the above will illustrate more satisfactorily that terminal elements never appear inside derivational stems:

(5.3) [(urb)$_n$ e]$_N$ 'city'
       [((urb)$_n$ an)$_a$ o]$_A$ 'urban'   (*urbeano)
       [(((urb)$_n$ an)$_a$ ism)$_n$ o]$_N$ 'city planning'   (*urbeanoismo)

       [(agu)$_n$ a]$_N$ 'water'
       [((agu)$_n$ os)$_a$ o]$_A$ 'watery'   (*aguaoso)
       [(((agu)$_n$ os)$_a$ idad)$_n$]$_N$ 'wateriness'   (*aguaosoidad)

       [(buen)$_a$ o]$_A$ 'good'
       [((bon)$_a$ dad)$_n$]$_N$ 'goodness'   (*bonodad)[2]
       [(((bon)$_a$ dad)$_n$ os)$_a$ o]$_A$ 'full of goodness' (*bonodadoso)

       [(lej)$_a$ os]$_A$ 'far (away)' (adv)
       [((lej)$_a$ an)$_a$ o]$_A$ 'distant' (adj)   (*lejosano)
       [(((lej)$_a$ an)$_a$ í)$_n$ a]$_N$ 'distance'   (*lejosanoía)

These two sets of examples are illustrative of the bulk of the suffixation process in the language—in which derivational suffixes attach to derivational stems (the constituent (...)$_x$) rather than to words (the constituent [...]$_x$).

The relatively rare case in which a suffix attaches at the word level rather than to derivational stems is exemplified most clearly with the adverb-forming -*mente:*

(5.4) *Adjective*   *Adverb*
      [(fuert)$_a$ e]$_A$ [[(fuert)$_a$ e]$_A$ mente]$_A$
      [(formal)$_a$]$_A$ [[(formal)$_a$]$_A$ mente]$_A$

As illustrated, a terminal element appears to the left of adverbial -*mente* if and only if the contained adjective has one. For historical reasons, -*mente* attaches to the feminine rather than the masculine adjective (if the two are distinct): *claramente* 'clearly', not **claromente*. This fact provides us with a useful test by which we can be sure that the vowel preceding -*mente* is indeed the terminal element rather than some otherwise unidentified "linking vowel." To the above-mentioned examples *fuerte(mente)* versus *formal(mente)*, which are themselves evidential in this respect, we may add adjectives like those in (5.5), in which the masculine has no terminal element but the feminine has -*a:*

(5.5) *Masculine*   *Feminine*   *Adverb*
    conservador   conservador_a_   conservadoramente
                                                'conservatively'
    holgazán   holgazan_a_   holgazanamente
                                                'lazily, idly'

*Conservadormente and **holgazánmente*, without terminal elements, are ill formed (for purely morphological reasons—they are phonologically and of course semantically impeccable). Thus, given that terminal elements appear only at the level of the word, it follows that adverbial -*mente* attaches to this constituent, not to the derivational stem.

The same is true of diminutive -*ito* and -*(e)cito*, although this fact is masked by certain complexities that have been studied elsewhere. (The most careful discussion that I know of is Jaeggli (1980).) Suffice it to say here that diminutivization must be able to "see" the terminal element of the base noun or adjective in order for the correct allomorph of the suffix to be chosen. This is clear from contrasting pairs like the following:

(5.6) *Base*   *Diminutive*
    [(cort)_n_ e]_N_   cort_ecito_ (*cort_ito_)   'cut'
    [(cort)_a_ o]_A_   cort_ito_ (*cort_ecito_)   'cut short'

It is now easy to see how the distinction between "word" and "derivational stem," and the suffixes that attach to each, provides a principled basis for describing the contrast between cyclically and noncyclically produced stress contours. If we simply recognize the word as the domain of stress assignment, the contrasts illustrated in section 4.3 follow automatically.[3] The next examples illustrate graphically which morphological bracketings do and do not constitute cyclic domains:

(5.7) *Yes*   *No*
 [[fuert e]$_A$ mente]$_A$ [[(fuert)$_a$ e]$_A$ mente]$_A$
 [[fuert e]$_A$ cit o]$_A$ [([(fuert)$_a$ e]$_A$ cit)$_A$ o]$_A$
 [urb an ism o]$_N$ [(((urb)$_n$ an)$_a$ ism)$_n$ o]$_N$
 [bon dad os o]$_A$ [(((bon)$_a$ dad)$_n$ os)$_a$ o]$_A$

The two exceptional suffixes that attach to words—adverbial -*mente* and the productive diminutive suffix—are those associated with cyclic stress in section 4.3, while the majority type suffixes (those dubbed "other" in section 4.3) that attach to derivational stems are those associated with noncyclic stress.

It is important to note that considerations having nothing to do with cyclicity also lead to the conclusion that the domain of stress rules in Spanish is not the "derivational stem" but rather the "word." In section 4.2.4 we saw that penultimate stress is the normal, "unmarked," case for vowel-final words, where *word* was implicitly understood in the technical sense given in the present section. That is, we took the stress rule for the case in question to be "Stress the penultimate syllable," understanding the domain of this rule to be [...]$_X$. If, on the other hand, we had formulated the statement about markedness in terms of the derivational stem (that is, if we had taken its domain to be $(...)_X$), then the rule would be "Stress the final syllable." There is good evidence that the former, not the latter, is the correct generalization. Consider first the case of disyllabic prepositions like *para, hasta, sobre*. Normally—that is, in nonmetalinguistic discourse—prepositions are stressless in Spanish; they are proclitics to their object. (Prepositions cannot be stranded in Spanish; there are no other nonmonosyllabic proclitics or enclitics.) When pronounced in isolation, however, in some artificial situation such as reading the sentence just above, they must have penultimate stress: *pára, hásta, sóbre* rather than **pará, *hastá, *sobré*. The latter are grotesquely unthinkable. Notice now that prepositions have no internal structure; in particular, they have no derivational stem (there is no deprepositional or adprepositional derivational morphology). It follows then that only the rule "Stress the penultimate syllable in the domain [...]$_X$" can account for the contour spontaneously and invariably given to prepositions pronounced in isolation. It might be countered that penultimate main stress of prepositions in isolation is (somehow) a reflection of their usual nonprimary stress in phrases, e.g., *pàra mí, hàsta mañána, sòbre la mésa*. Whatever the merits of this proposal may be in the case of prepositions, it is in principle inapplicable to cases like the following. Many speakers use the device of apocope to form nonce hypocoristics. For example, *profesór* becomes *prófĕ*, *arquitécto* becomes *árquĭ*, *muñéca* becomes *múñĕ*, *Maurício* becomes *Máurĭ*, and so on. The apocopated forms invariably have penultimate stress, regardless of the contour of the source words. Therefore, there is no possibility that the stress of the former might be somehow parasitic on the latter. The nonce forms clearly have no internal structure (in particular, no derivational stem). Therefore, the stress rule that speakers must be applying productively and spontaneously is "Stress the penultimate syllable in the domain [...]$_X$," where X identifies the level of the "word" as I have defined it in this section.

Perhaps a discussion of stress contours such as (cyclic) *formàlménte* versus (noncyclic) *fòrmalísmo* provides an appropriate context for comment on a conceptual point which has caused some difficulty in studies of stress rules in Spanish. The examples just cited suffice to show that neither of the arrangements σὸσόσ (*formàlménte*) or ὸσόσσ (*fòrmalísmo*) is possible or impossible in an absolute sense. Rather, each is well formed or not with respect to a certain morphological structure. Analogous remarks hold for primary stress. For example, it is true that primary stress cannot occur left of the antepenultimate syllable in nouns and adjectives—recall **átapama*, etc., in section 4.2.3. It does not follow, however, that arrangements such as Xόσσσ are "unpronounceable" in the same sense as, say, words with prohibited consonant clusters and/or exotic vowels, e.g., *[tŋámxr], *[lʌdɔ́p]. In fact, words with three or (in the extreme case) four syllables following the primary stress exist and do not tax the speaker's speech production mechanisms, e.g., *examinándŏsĕlŏs, castígŭesĕmĕlŏ*. The last word is

$$\text{examinándŏsĕlŏs} \atop {\scriptstyle 1\ 2\ 3} \qquad \text{castígŭesĕmĕlŏ} \atop {\scriptstyle 1\ 2\ \ 3\ 4}$$

composed of the imperative verb form *castígue* plus the three clitics *se, me, lo,* which do not "count" in stress placement. The point of these remarks is that, clearly, stress rules cannot be viewed as statements about pronunciation. Rather, they are well-formedness conditions on arrangements of prominence with respect to specific morphological configurations.

5.1.2 Prosodic Representations: A First Pass
As a basis for further discussion and refinement, I will begin to record some of the observations of the previous sections in the form of prosodic trees (see the references in note 1 of chapter 4). I will adopt certain conventions, which are illustrated in the following structures:

(5.8) a.   [gramàticàlidád]   b.   [gèneratív]o

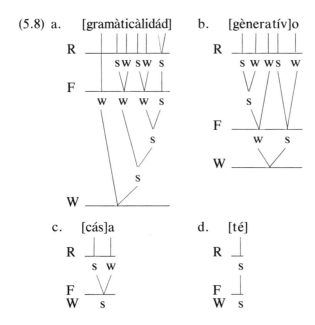

c.   [cás]a   d.   [té]

For the sake of visual clarity, morphological structure internal to the derivational stem is ignored (e.g., ((((gramat)ic)al)i + dad)$_n$), the derivational stem is bracketed, and the brackets are left unlabeled where confusion is not likely to result. Primary word stress is marked with an acute accent, and nonprimary stresses of any degree are marked with a grave accent. This information is of course redundant given the prosodic tree drawn below the segmental string, but it is included for easy reference.

R indicates the rhyme level, F the foot level, and W the word level. Assuming the above examples to be typical, we can see that in Spanish the following statements hold:

(5.9) a. *Foot* trees are left-branching, labeled s (w). (Nonbranching

nodes are labeled at the level of the word.)

    b. *Word* trees are right-branching, labeled (w) s.

This minimal specification of the properties of prosodic trees in Spanish will of course be elaborated as we proceed, but these statements by themselves indicate what is wrong with certain ill-formed configurations illustrated in section 4.2.5. For example:

(5.10) a. *[Panàmá]   b.   *[gràmàticàlidád]

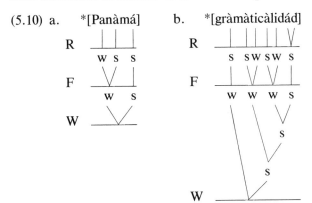

Panàmá has a foot incorrectly labeled *w s;* reversing this to *s w* gives a correct representation of *Pànamá*. *Gràmàticàlidád* has an initial nonbranching foot node illicitly labeled *s;* removal of this label gives the correct tree, shown in (5.8).

5.1.3 Extrametricality
I introduce here a theoretical notion that will be seen to play an important role in Spanish stress assignment.[4] I will use Spanish words to illustrate the device of *extrametricality* in the present section, but since justification for the appeal to this mechanism is developed only later, the examples presented immediately below can simply be taken as hypothetical cases.

An element that is extrametrical with respect to a particular representation is ignored by the rules that apply to that representation, as though the element were not there. I will use the symbol " / ", printed as an overstrike, to mark segments as extrametrical in segmental strings, and "–" to indicate extrametricality in the corresponding rhyme. Thus, if the *i* of *métrico* is to be represented as extrametrical, I will write

(5.11) métri̸co
        | ⟊ |

The rules of Spanish then produce the following prosodic tree:

(5.12)   [métrịc]o

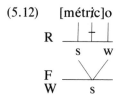

Extrametrical elements must eventually be incorporated into prosodic structure. This is accomplished by *Stray Rhyme Adjunction*, which can be stated as follows:

(5.13) "Adjoin a stray rime as a recessive [weak] node of an adjacent foot."   (Hayes (1980, 159))

Stray Rhyme Adjunction converts the representation of *métrico* shown above to the following:

(5.14)   [métrịc]o

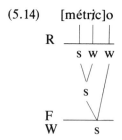

Note that Stray Rhyme Adjunction is "structure preserving" in the sense that it always applies so that syllable and foot structures maintain their normal directionality of branching and labeling of elements as *s* or *w*. In our example, this property guarantees that the redrawn foot tree of *métrico* is left-branching and labeled (*s*, *w*), as all foot trees in Spanish must be.

The example of *métrico* illustrates a further, apparently universal, characteristic of extrametrical elements, namely, that they are always peripheral in the constituents in which they appear, in the relevant representation (cf. Hayes (1980, 118, 134)). It is easy to see that the extrametrical *i* of (5.15) is the right-peripheral rhyme in the derivational stem in which it appears.

(5.15)   [métrịc]o

It is important to bear in mind that Stray Rhyme Adjunction is a universal convention rather than a phonological rule. It applies wherever possible after language-particular tree construction rules have applied. Stray Rhyme Adjunction is constrained by its own theory, that of extrametricality, not by language-particular restrictions.

5.2 A New Synthesis

At the level of description, the next task is to provide an analysis that gives a descriptively adequate account of the new data in section 4.4 without sacrificing any of the correct generalizations formulated in existing descriptions on the basis of the material outlined in sections 4.2 and 4.3. After a brief comment on markedness, I will follow the order of topics in section 4.2, starting with "prosodic restrictions," into which I will intercalate new material from section 4.4 as the relevant generalizations are uncovered.

5.2.1 Markedness as Extrametricality

This section will provide a minimal introduction to the representation of marked and unmarked stress patterns in the lexicon and the mapping of these representations into prosodic trees. This introduction will facilitate the discussion of several points in the following sections, after which I will return to the topic of markedness to examine certain questions of detail.

Section 4.2 established that information must be supplied in the lexicon regarding the status of the stress of individual items as marked or unmarked. Exactly how is this lexical information represented? At least two of the proposals of Harris (1975) still seem to be well motivated and essentially correct though in need of reinterpretation in terms of prosodic theory.

One of these proposals is that lexical markedness information regarding stress must be registered in the lexicon as a fact about derivational stems, not as a fact about a particular set of affixes (say, terminal elements) or as a fact about words as a whole. To illustrate with a specific example, the fact that the word *sábana* has a marked stress pattern must be recorded lexically by a representation essentially like [(saban)$_n$ a]$_N$—where I arbitrarily choose underlining to identify the constituent in which markedness lodges—not like [(saban)$_n$ a]$_N$ or [(saban)$_n$ a]$_N$. To see that this must be the case, consider first the fact

that there are sets of words which have identical morphological constituency but different stress patterns. For example, *sábana* and *sabána* both consist of a derivational stem plus the terminal element -*a*. It
would be incoherent to say that this -*a*, one and the same morpheme in
both words, is lexically marked in one but lexically unmarked in the
other. Therefore, the difference in stress in *sábana* and *sabána* can
only be attributed to the stems: as [(saban) a] versus [(saban) a]. Consider next near-minimal pairs like *césped* versus *mercéd*, both of which
consist of a single morpheme, the derivational stem. Here, obviously,
nothing other than the derivational stem exists to which the stress contrast might be attributed. The remaining piece of the argument comes
from sets of words that have identical derivational stems but different
terminal elements, like the following:

(5.16) múltiple   (adj)   'multiple (contusions)'
       múltiplo   (noun)   '(4 is a) multiple (of 2)'

       alemána   (noun, adj) 'German' (feminine)
       alemán_   (noun, adj) 'German' (masculine)

       síncopa   (noun)   'syncopation', 'syncope' (grammar)
       síncope   (noun)   'syncope' (medicine)

(The number of examples of this sort is enormous; in fact, every ordinary masculine/feminine adjective pair like *bonita/bonito* is a relevant
case.) In each such set, the members all regularly have the same
(marked or unmarked) stress pattern. Clearly, then, the derivational
stem is the constant factor in determining the stress pattern. This generalization would be lost if anything other than the stem were the
bearer of the relevant lexical mark. In particular, if whole words were
marked, it would be completely accidental that sets like *{múltiple,
multíplo}*, *{alémana, alemán}*, *{boníta, bónito}*, etc., are not found.

The second proposal is that the terms *unmarked* and *marked* stress be
taken literally, that is, as the absence and presence, respectively, of
special information about stress in lexical entries. This is illustrated in
the following typical vowel-final words, where stress on the penultimate syllable is the unmarked case.

(5.17) *Unmarked*   *Marked*
       pomáda = /pomada/   nómada = /nomada/
       hebréo = /ebreo/   áureo = /aureo/
       obóe   = /oboe/   héroe = /eroe/

Prosodic structure assignment in the unmarked case is straightforward, exactly as illustrated in section 5.1.2.

(5.18) a. [pomád]a   b. [hebré]o   c. [obó]e

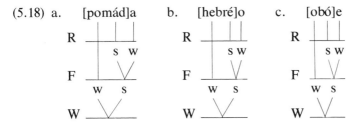

It is no accident that the slash symbol used in section 5.1.3 to indicate extrametrical segments is chosen here to represent marked stress in the lexicon. The claim is that the two are one and the same phenomenon. If this is correct—and evidence that it is will mount as we proceed—then in the case of marked stress, prosodic structure is assigned as follows:

(5.19)   [nómad]a   →   [nómad]a

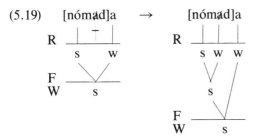

The arrow indicates the effect of Stray Rhyme Adjunction; thus, the comments about assignment of prosodic structure to *métrico* in the preceding section carry over intact to the present example.

A brief digression is in order, to comment on certain metrical conventions of Spanish verse. Consider the following line of poetry:

(5.20) Mientras se olviden los árboles   (Cernuda)
        1   2   3   4 5 6 7 8 9

We can easily count (at least) nine syllables, but this line scans as octosyllabic. By convention, the proparoxytone *árboles* counts as disyllabic; one of its syllables is metrically irrelevant, i.e., "extrametrical." Interestingly, the extrametrical syllable is the penult. The following examples (from Real Academia Española (1973, 62–63)) show that this is so:

(5.21) *á-e:*   á<u>ng</u>el   *rhymes (assonates) with*   árbol<u>e</u>s, háb<u>i</u>les
      á-a: sá<u>l</u>va   fábul<u>a</u>, cerám<u>i</u>ca
      á-o: prá<u>do</u>   ángul<u>o</u>, elást<u>ico</u>
      é-a: tré<u>nza</u>   cédul<u>a</u>, intrép<u>ida</u>
      é-e: vé<u>ce</u>s   célib<u>e</u>, acércal<u>e</u>
      í-a: mí<u>ra</u>   vísper<u>a</u>s, retícul<u>a</u>
      etc.

Clearly the vowel quality, and indeed even the presence, of the penultimate syllable of proparoxytones is irrelevant in the metrical tradition under discussion. This can fairly be regarded as remarkable corroboration for the proposals made here concerning markedness and extrametricality, according to which it is exactly the same syllable that contains the lexical mark of extrametricality.

Returning now to the main thread of the exposition, markedness in consonant-final words is also characterized as extrametricality. For example:

(5.22) *Unmarked*   *Marked*
      esquimál = /eskimal/   caníbal = /kanibal̸/
      paréd   = /pared/   huésped = /wesped̸/
      mujér   = /muxer/   cráter   = /krater̸/

In the unmarked case, prosodic structure is assigned as follows:

(5.23) a.   [èskimál]   b.   [paréd]

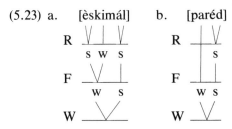

A constraint which I will explore in detail below prevents construction of trees like the following:

(5.24) a.   *[eskímal]   b.   *[páred]

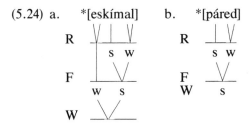

The illegal subconfigurations here are (5.25a,b); as we shall see, the rules of Spanish do not allow branching foot-nodes labeled *w*.

(5.25) a. -al   b. -ed

    $\bigvee$ $\bigvee$

     w   w

Now consider the marked case in consonant-final words, for example, *caníbal* and *cráter:*

(5.26) a.   [caníbaɬ]   b.   [crátei̯]

Notice first that extrametrical -*l* and -*r* are the rightmost rhyme elements in the derivational stem, thus permissible (peripheral) extrametrical segments. The prohibition against branching weak foot-nodes just mentioned cannot "see" this extrametrical segment. Thus, since the final rhyme (5.27a,b) is nonbranching as far as the prosodic rules can see,

(5.27) a. -al   b. -er

    $\bigvee$ $\bigvee$

the last two rhymes in each word can be collected into binary *s w* feet

              $\bigvee$

in the normal fashion illustrated in section 5.1.2.

What is the role of Stray Rhyme Adjunction in this last pair of examples? The extrametrical consonant is not actually "stray," since it is already incorporated into rhyme structure by the rules of syllable formation, and its rhyme in turn is incorporated into foot structure via its nuclear vowel. This case is thus significantly different from that of *métrico, nómada,* etc., in which the extrametrical segment has no link with the prosodic tree until Stray Rhyme Adjunction provides one. Notice, however, that the extrametrical consonant in *caníbal, huésped, cráter,* etc., is the metrically weak element in its rhyme, which is congruent with the "structure-preserving" property of Stray Rhyme Adjunction mentioned in section 5.1.3. (In this regard, see note 9.)

Section 4.2.4 makes two statements concerning the relative markedness of stress patterns in Spanish: (a) penultimate stress is unmarked in vowel-final words, and (b) final stress is unmarked in consonant-final words. Obviously, it would be better to have one statement, reflecting a single generalization. We have in fact achieved this generalization: marked stress is indicated in the lexicon in all cases as extrametricality of the rightmost rhyme segment in the derivational stem.

It should perhaps be emphasized once more that Stray Rhyme Adjunction is not a rule of Spanish but rather a universal convention that automatically adjusts the output of language-particular tree construction rules. The operation of Stray Syllable Adjunction is thus "cost free" in a description of Spanish. Furthermore, insofar as the details of Spanish stress patterns are associated with the theory of extrametricality, the apparent vagaries of Spanish prosodic structure can be seen to follow not from language-particular stipulations but rather from universal grammar.

5.2.2 The Major Prosodic Restriction
The first prosodic restriction mentioned in section 4.2.3 is stated as follows: "Stress must fall on one of the last three syllables of the word." How do we translate this prose statement into terms of prosodic tree structure? In fact, most of the necessary elements are already included in the "first pass" through prosodic representations in section 5.1.2, where, in particular, it is stipulated that word trees in Spanish are right-branching structures labeled (w, s). Since this stipulation guarantees that the rightmost foot of a word is the strongest—i.e., contains the primary stress—we can control the position of primary stress by controlling the size of the rightmost foot. Specifically, given the stipulation in section 5.1.2 that foot trees are left-branching structures labeled (s, w), we must limit the inventory of feet that can be constructed at the right edge of a word to the following:

(5.28) a. s   b. s   w   c. s   w   w

How this is to be done can best be appreciated by considering examples like these:

(5.29) *A*   *B*   *C*
[déspøt]a   [despøt + ísm]o   [despøt + íc]o
[númₑr]o   [numₑr + ós]o   [numₑr + íc]o
[ídøl]o   [idøl + átr + í]a   [idøl + átr]a
[hérø]e   [herø + ín]a   [herø + íc]o

The antepenultimate stress of the words in column A means, on this account, that the final vowel of the derivational stem is extrametrical, as shown. (Prosodic structure is thus assigned to these words as illustrated above with *métrico, nómada,* etc.) This vowel is the rightmost rhyme element in the derivational stem in the words in column A, thus "peripheral" in its morphological domain and consequently a legitimately extrametrical segment. Not so in the words in column B, where every extrametrical segment is separated from the edge of the derivational stem by at least one segment on the rhyme level:

(5.30) a. [despøt + ísm]o   b. [numₑr + ós]o

c. [idøl + átr + í]a   d. [herø + ín]a

Similarly, in column C the extrametrical segments in the derivational suffixes are all adjacent to the right edge of the derivational stem and thus legitimately extrametrical, but the extrametrical segments in the root morphemes are all nonperipheral. As observed in section 5.1.3, it seems to be universally true that extrametrical elements are peripheral, that is, not separated from the edges of their morphological domains by any other element on the same level of representation. For ease of reference, I will name this observation the *Peripherality Condition* and formulate it somewhat more explicitly as follows:

(5.31) *Peripherality Condition*

$$a \rightarrow a \ / \ [_\Sigma \ X \ \underline{\quad} \ Y \ b \ Z]_\Sigma$$

On the intended interpretation, the Peripherality Condition does not simply prohibit assignment of extrametricality in the lexicon to some element a if a is followed by another element b on the same level of representation in the same domain; rather, this condition actually erases the extrametricality mark of a under the conditions specified, though a may be legitimately extrametrical in other contexts. Thus, the Peripherality Condition automatically adjusts [despøt + ism]o to [despot + ism]o, [despøt + ic]o to [despot + ic]o, [idøl + atr + i]a to [idol + atr + i]a, and so on. It is easy to see that the Peripherality Condition permits at most one extrametrical segment at the right edge of the derivational stem in Spanish, as in [despot + ic]o. It follows, then, given the procedure for prosodic tree construction suggested earlier, that the largest foot that can appear at the right edge of a word in Spanish is the one shown in (5.32),

(5.32)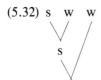

and thus that primary stress can never appear to the left of the antepenultimate syllable. In short, no ad hoc stipulation is needed in the grammar of Spanish to enforce the prosodic restriction under discussion.[5]

It may seem at first glance that the operation of the universal Peripherality Condition in conjunction with the Spanish-particular tree construction procedure is exactly equivalent to the prose statement "Stress must fall on one of the last three syllables of the word." In fact, however, the two formulations have slightly different consequences. I will now consider two cases in which the Peripherality Condition makes better predictions than the prose statement does. I know of no case in which the converse is true.

Notice first that the new formulation rules out not only words like preantepenultimately stressed *átapana but also antepenultimately stressed words of the form *átapan, with no terminal element. That is, stress must be on one of the last two syllables of words having no terminal element. On the analysis proposed here, the position of stress in the type *átapan requires that both segments of the final rhyme -an be extrametrical:

(5.33)   [atapan]   →   [atapan]

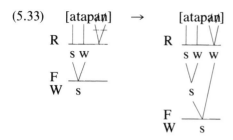

(The arrow represents the operation of Stray Rhyme Adjunction.) However, the Peripherality Condition prohibits such a configuration of extrametrical segments, and therefore characterizes *átapan as deviant. This is apparently correct, since there is only one generally current word of the type *átapan, namely, régimen, which is not only unique with regard to stress placement but also deviant in other respects.[6] The prose statement "Stress must fall on one of the last three syllables of the word," on the other hand, says nothing about this type of word since stress in fact does fall on one of the last three syllables. Deviant *átapan is thus lumped together with well-formed proparoxytones like sábana, ídolo, héroe, etc. This must be counted as a point in favor of the new formulation, which is more restrictive than the traditional prose statement. This statement is shown to be insufficiently restrictive by the following case as well.

In section 4.4.2 I discussed a generalization that does not follow from and cannot be integrated into previous analyses, namely, that "Final syllables with prevocalic glides exclude antepenultimate stress." Examples like the following provide an interesting angle from which to examine this generalization further:

(5.34) [aristócrat]a   [aristocrác + i]a
        [demócrat]a   [democrác + i]a
        [sacríleg]o   [sacriég + i]o
        [présbit]a   [presbíc + i]a
        [benéfic]o   [benefíc + i]o
        [cántabr]o   [Cantábr + i]a
        [adúlter]o   [adultér + i]o
        [polígam]o   [poligám + i]a
        [náufrag]o   [naufrág + i]o
        [bárbar]o   [barbár + i]e
        [párroc]o   [parróqu + i]a
        [mártir]   [martír + i]o
        [míser]o   [misér + i]a

As previously mentioned, words like *míseria, *mártirio, etc., are unacceptable, despite mísero, mártir, etc. The position of stress in the unacceptable words requires that the last two rhyme segments of the derivational stem be extrametrical:

(5.35)   [misǝr + i̯]a   →   [misǝr + i̯]a

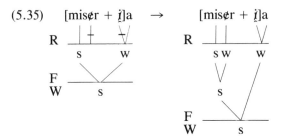

(The arrow represents the operation of Stray Rhyme Adjunction.) Again, the Peripherality Condition prohibits such a configuration of extrametrical segments and therefore characterizes *míseria, etc., as deviant. (This case is just like *átapan except that in *míseria the two extrametrical segments are in different rhymes while in *átapan they are in the same rhyme.) This is apparently correct. I can find only one counterexample, namely, the stem of ventrílocuo and grandílocuo, whose idiosyncrasy is evident in view of the existence of well-behaved altilócuo and maquilócuo. Unlike the Peripherality Condition, the statement "Stress must fall on one of the last three syllables of the word" says nothing about the oddity of ventrílocuo, which is not distinguished from ordinary proparoxytones like bárbaro, demócrata, etc. It is a significant success for the Peripherality Condition that it subsumes under a single generalization the deviance of both *átapan and *míseria, which are unrelated and intractable in previous analyses.

5.2.3 The Second Prosodic Restriction
The second prosodic restriction mentioned in section 4.2.3 is "Antepenultimate stress is impossible if the penult is a closed syllable." It is important to bear in mind that this statement does not discriminate simply between unmarked and marked stress placement but rather between well-formed and ill-formed contours.

In studies not grounded on an explicit theory of syllable structure—which includes all of the work on Spanish stress of which I am aware—the restriction in question is enforced by a rule or rules that, in effect, prohibit the following configuration:

(5.36) $*\ldots\acute{V}C_0VC_2VC_0$

That is, "Antepenultimate stress is impossible if the penultimate vowel is followed by two or more consonants." This formulation, however, runs afoul of well-formed examples like *múltiple, idólatra, fúnebre*, and many more. Accordingly, previous studies have modified the constraint shown above to allow antepenultimate stress if the second consonant of the C_2 cluster is a liquid. It is easy to see, however, that this move is necessitated by the failure to take syllable structure into account. The relevant difference between, say, *múltiple* and **cáramba* is that the penult of the former is open while that of the latter is closed: *múlti-ple* versus **cáram-ba*. Given an explicit account of syllable structure that provides a representation of the structure of rhymes,[7] as a minimal step in the right direction we may express as follows the configuration that is ruled out by the prosodic restriction now under discussion:

(5.37) $*\ldots\acute{V}C_0VCC_0VC_0$

$$\bigvee$$

R

This formulation obviously draws the distinction that we are seeking between ill-formed (5.38a) with a closed penult, and well-formed (5.38b,c), etc., with open penults.

(5.38) a. *cáramba   b. múlt i ple   c. idól a tra

V | |V |V

R O   R O   R O

It was observed in section 4.4.1 that not only consonants but also glides may not close penults in antepenultimately stressed words. For example, **cára[i]ba* and **cára[u]ba* are as bad as **cáramba*. Crucially, "bad" does not mean "accidentally missing," perhaps for historical reasons; rather, native speakers vigorously reject words of the type under discussion as impermissible. We may easily account for these additional data by simply generalizing the formulation of restriction (5.37) to the following:

(5.39) $*\ldots\acute{V}C_0xyC_0VC_0$

$$\bigvee$$

R

At the same time, I will restate this restriction in purely syllabic terms, without otherwise altering its content:

(5.40) *Ŕ R R
       /\
       x y

That is, "Antepenultimate stress is impossible if the penultimate rhyme branches." This generalization has consequences, namely, it rules out not only rhymes of the form VG but also those of the form GV. This is exactly right. As mentioned in section 4.4.1, words like *sos*[i]*égo, framb*[u]*ésa* are well formed while **sós*[i]*ego, *frámb*[u]*esa* are not. Since the indicated glides are rhyme elements (see note 6 of chapter 4), the new formulation makes the right distinctions in all cases. For example:

(5.41) *sósiego
        | \/ |
       *Ŕ R R

I have changed the vocabulary of the restriction from a statement made in terms of segmental strings to one made in terms of rhyme structure, with the desirable consequences already noted. In so doing, I have almost given a reformulation in terms of prosodic tree structure; and I will finish that job now. The salient fact is illustrated in the following examples:

(5.42) a.   b.   *[sósieg]o
                              ||
                            *[sóseig]o
                              ||
        [fúnebr]e   *[sóseng]o

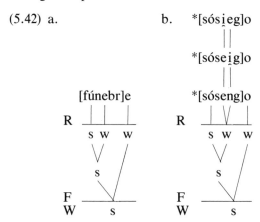

In short, the only difference between the two prosodic trees is that the ill-formed structure contains the substructure (5.43).

(5.43)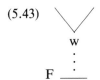

I thus propose the *Branching Condition* as part of the procedure for assigning prosodic structure in Spanish:

(5.44) *Branching Condition*
  Foot-nodes labeled *w*(eak) cannot branch.

Since the Branching Condition is in a clear sense "context free," it is the maximally general reformulation of the original prose statement "Antepenultimate stress is impossible if the penult is a closed sylla- ble."[8] What are the consequences of this final generalization, whereby the prosodic structure surrounding the focal branching node becomes irrelevant? Clearly, this final version makes the right distinctions in all of the cases discussed so far. To see the consequences in other cases requires investigating the interaction of the Branching Condition with markedness, interpreted as extrametricality. This is the topic of the next section.

5.2.4 Markedness Revisited
In the introductory comments on marked stress patterns in section 5.2.1 I alluded to the Branching Condition, without stating or naming it, in the discussion of consonant-final words like unmarked *sutíl* versus marked *útil*. Prosodic trees of the following sort played a role in that discussion:

(5.45) a. [sutíl]   b. [útil]   c. *[útil]

R ___ s   R ___ s w   R ___ s w

F ___ w s   F ___ W s   F ___ W s

W ___

In the case of *sutíl,* the rightmost foot-node is labeled *s* and thus may branch without violating the Branching Condition. *Útil* also does not violate the Branching Condition, which cannot "see" the extrametrical right branch of the final rhyme. The representation *[*útil*], on the other hand, does violate the condition, as shown, and is therefore ill formed.

If the device of extrametricality can thus "outwit" the Branching Condition in cases like *útil,* we must verify that maneuvers with this device are not available that might undermine the desirable consequences of the Branching Condition displayed in the previous section. The following words will illustrate the relevant cases: *Sàlamánca* versus **Salámanca, Màracá*[i̱]*bo* versus **Maráca*[i̱]*bo, Vènez*[u̱]*éla* versus **Venéz*[u̱]*ela.* The prosodic tree of *Sàlamánca* is constructed in the now familiar way:

(5.46)   [Sàlamánc]a

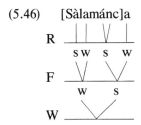

The tree associated with ill-formed **Salámanca* violates the Branching Condition since the branching rhyme *an* is dominated by a weak foot-node:

(5.47)   *[Salámanc]a

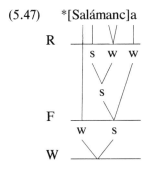

The next step is to verify that there is no way to construct a well-formed tree for **Salámanca* by invoking extrametricality, specifically, by making *an* a nonbranching rhyme:

(5.48) a.   [Salamanc]a   b.   [Salamanc]a

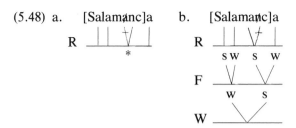

As shown, no tree can be constructed for *Salamanca* since the Peripherality Condition immediately aborts the rhyme representation in
which nonextrametrical *n* intervenes between extrametrical *a* and the
edge of the derivational stem. (More accurately, the Peripherality Condition erases the mark of extrametricality on the *a*, so that the result is
inevitably *Sàlamánca*.) Next, the representation *Salamaṇca* does not
result in *Salámaṇca because the extrametricality of *ṇ* is ineffectual; a
normal (*s*, *w*) foot (5.49) is constructed over -*aṇca* by the normal procedure that has been illustrated several times above.

(5.49) -aṇca

Again, the only possible result is *Sàlamánca*. It is easy to see that
Maracaibo, Venezuela (5.50a,b) would suffer the same fate as *Salamanca* (5.48a), and that *Maracaibo, Venezuela* (5.51a,b) would turn out
like *Salamaṇca* (5.48b), with penultimate stress in all cases despite the
extrametrical elements.[9]

(5.50) a. [Maracaib]o   b. [Venezuel]a

(5.51) a. [Maracaib]o   b. [Venezuel]a

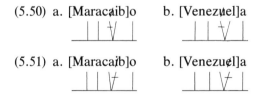

In short, the machinery involving extrametricality that we have set up
is sufficiently constrained so that it cannot subvert the Branching Condition in any of the cases considered.[10]

Let us return now to cases like *sutíl* versus *útil*. As stated in section
4.2.4, consonant-final oxytones like *sutíl* and paroxytones like *útil* are
uncontroversially regarded as unmarked and marked, respectively. On
the view of markedness with respect to stress as extrametricality, as

sketched in section 5.2.1, words like these are represented in the lexicon as [sutil] versus [uti̱l]. We will see now how these proposals fare as
more data are brought into the picture.

As a consequence of constraints on rhyme structure, Spanish words
ending in consonant clusters are relatively rare. (See the discussion at
several points in part I.) They are restricted mostly to a few proper
names like *Guitárt, Tiánt* (both of Catalan origin) and common nouns
like *vals* and a few others. Native speakers reject penultimately
stressed cluster-final (hypothetical) words like **Guítart, *ávals.* Oxytones like *Guitárt* and monosyllabic *vals* obviously do not violate the
Branching Condition, since their (rightmost or only) branching foot-
node is strong:

(5.52) a.   [Guitárt]   b.   [vals]

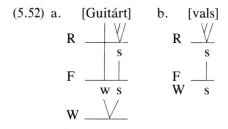

Forms like **Guítart, *ávals,* on the other hand, do violate this condition, even if the final consonant is lexically marked as extrametrical:

(5.53) a.   *[Guítart̸]   b.   *[ávals̸]

Only lexical entries like [Guitart̸], [avals̸] can circumvent the Branching
Condition, but these in turn cannot survive the Peripherality Condition,
which would automatically convert them to [Guitart̸], [avals̸]. Small
wonder, then, that native speakers reject paroxytones that end in consonant clusters. Yet there do exist a few words like *bíceps, Sáenẕ, tórax̱*
(phonetically *tóra*[ks]). Why should these not be rejected as well? An
answer reveals itself when we take morphological structure into account. The crucial difference is this:

(5.54) [vals] *vs.* [torak]s

As shown, the final -*s* of [vals] is inside the derivational stem, while that of [torak]s is outside this morphological constituent. This is not a magical invocation of morphology. Exactly this difference in morphological structure is independently motivated by the plurals *valses* versus *tórax* (*sic*, not **tóraxes*), derived forms like *torác* + *ico* (not **toráx* + *ico*), and other evidence.[11] Recognizing the fact that *tórax* is morphologically [torak]s allows us to capture the following generalization: consonants outside the derivational stem are predictably extrametrical. I will give this generalization the name *Predictable Extrametricality* and state it somewhat more precisely as follows:[12]

(5.55) *Predictable Extrametricality*

$$C \rightarrow \mathcal{C} \; / \; [(\ldots)_x \; Z \; \underline{\quad\quad} \;]_x$$

Given the morphological structure [(torak)$_n$ s]$_N$, the -*s* is predictably extrametrical: [(torak)$\cancel{s}$]. Notice that we are free to mark a segment inside the derivational stem as idiosyncratically, unpredictably, extrametrical: [(tora$\cancel{k}$)$\cancel{s}$]. The Peripherality Condition lets both of these marks stand since they are in different morphemes, one inside and one outside the derivational stem. The following prosodic tree can thus be assigned to *tórax* without violating either the Peripherality Condition or the Branching Condition:

(5.56)   [tórak]$\cancel{s}$

On the other hand, there is no conceivable motivation for postulating other than a monomorphemic structure for *Guitart, Tiant,* etc., whose prosodic structure must therefore be as shown above.

The position of the -*s* of [torak]s just outside the derivational stem is of course the position of the morphological unit we have called the terminal element. In fact, we may as well regard this -*s* as a special subtype of terminal element, an affiliation shared by the -*is* of words like *dósis, tésis, sífilis,* the -*es* of words like *diabétes, isósceles, Sócrates,* and the -*os* of words like *lejos, caos*.[13] (Words of this sort were mentioned in section 4.2.4.) Given that these suffixes function like terminal elements rather than derivational affixes, the class of words in question falls into place immediately in our analysis. In particular, their derivational stems may have marked or unmarked stress indicated in the lexicon, just like any other noun or adjective. For example:

(5.57) *Unmarked*   *Marked*
[encefalít]iş   [análįs]iş
[diabét]eş   [génҽs]iş
[neurós]iş   [metrópøl]iş
[hipnós]iş   [ósmøs]iş
[oás]iş   [prótąs]iş

In both unmarked and marked cases, prosodic trees are constructed without deviating in any way from the procedure that has been illustrated repeatedly above. For example:

(5.58) *Unmarked*   *Marked*

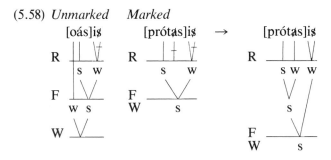

(Again, the arrow represents the operation of Stray Rhyme Adjunction.)

I have not yet taken a stand on vowel-final oxytones like *papá, café, israelí, dominó, Perú,* which, as mentioned in section 4.2.4, have caused difficulties for previous descriptions. It is not hard to see why. Vowel-final oxytones are clearly more "marked" in an intuitive sense than vowel-final paroxytones (e.g., *dominó* versus unmarked *molíno*). Yet in the technical sense, the category of marked stress in vowel-final words has been preempted by proparoxytones (e.g., *cómico*), and for uncontroversially good reasons. Now, how can three terms—*dominó, molíno,* and *cómico*—be squeezed into the binary marked–unmarked opposition?

Obviously, *papá* must differ from unmarked *pápa, dominó* from unmarked *molíno,* and so on, in some fundamental way. Grasping at a straw, we might assume that as a lexical peculiarity the words in question are assigned a branching rhyme on the final syllable. For example:

(5.59) a. papa   b. domino   c. Peru

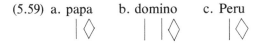

Thus, to avoid a violation of the Branching Condition, this final syllable can be dominated only by a strong rhyme-node:

(5.60) a.   papá   b.   dominó   c.   Perú

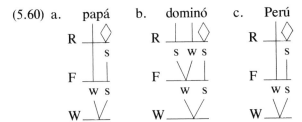

This proposal, however, enjoys no advantage that I can detect over the brute-force approach of simply assigning the requisite strong foot-node directly in the lexicon, thus:

(5.61) a. papa   b. domino   c. Peru

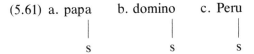

These lexically supplied node labels would be respected as further prosodic structure is assigned, so that the only possible outcome is the desired one:

(5.62) a.   papá   b.   dominó   c.   Perú

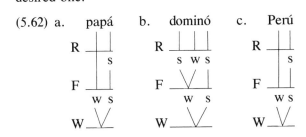

This second proposal avoids pointless moves but it ignores the crucial fact that final stress in *papá, café,* etc., is actually predictable. The "fundamental way" in which these words differ from *pápa, molíno,* etc., is that the former lack terminal elements. The morphological structures differ in the following way:[14]

(5.63) [dominó]   *vs.*   [molín]o
       [papá]   [páp]a
       [café]   [bás]e

The strong rightmost foot-node is thus not an idiosyncrasy of individual items that must be marked as such in the lexicon. Rather, it can be supplied by rule. The following formulation is sufficiently precise in the present context:

(5.64) *Strong Foot Rule*

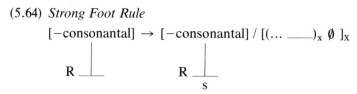

The Strong Foot Rule says that a nonconsonantal segment immediately adjacent to the right edge of the derivational stem is dominated by a strong foot-node if the derivational stem is not followed by a terminal element. The specification [−consonantal] correctly excludes from the domain of the rule all types of consonantal segments: liquids (*árbol*, *éter*), nasals (*jóven*), and obstruents (*huésped*). In short, I propose that vowel-final oxytones are unmarked in the technical sense, like vowel-final paroxytones (and unlike vowel-final proparoxytones). That is, words like *papá,* etc., carry no special lexical information relating specifically to stress. Such words are peculiar, however; they have vowel-final derivational stems not followed by a terminal element. The more usual pattern is that of words like [mar + e]a, [cano]a, [dese]o, etc., which do have a terminal element after a vowel-final derivational stem. It is thus gratuitous to attribute specifically to a marked stress pattern—as has been done previously, with consequent formal problems, as noted above—the odd feel and statistical infrequency of vowel-final oxytones.

The Strong Foot Rule provides an unexpected bonus, in the form of a principled solution to an outstanding problem. It was pointed out in section 4.4.2 that glide-final words must be stressed on the final syllable.[15] For example:

(5.65) *Well-formed*   *Ill-formed*
        convóy   *cónvoy
        caréy   *cárey
        Abréu   *Ábreu

Words with final consonantal segments can have either final or penultimate stress, as the unmarked and marked cases, respectively (*faról* vs. *árbol, ayér* vs. *éter, sartén* vs. *jóven, mercéd* vs. *huésped,* etc.).

Why is it, then, that no unmarked case—i.e., penultimate stress—is available for glide-final words? The answer is obvious now. Glide-final words have no terminal element, and their derivational stem ends in a [−consonantal] segment. Therefore, in accordance with the Strong Foot Rule, their rightmost rhyme must be dominated by a strong foot-node, thus:

(5.66) a.   [caréi]   b.   [Abréu]

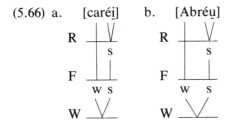

It is easy to see that this remains the case even if the final glide is marked as extrametrical. In sum, the Strong Foot Rule is not motivated solely by a relatively small subset of somewhat aberrant words like *papá, mamá, papú, zulú,* etc.; rather, it states what we can now recognize as one of the major prosodic regularities of Spanish.

5.3 Summary and Amplification

We have now covered all of the cases mentioned in sections 4.2 through 4.4, as well as a few others. It is time to summarize the proposals scattered throughout the foregoing sections, adding a few details whose earlier introduction might have overburdened the exposition. In the second part of the section I take a closer look at the prosodic cycle in Spanish.

5.3.1 Prosodic Tree Construction
The derivations in table 5.1 illustrate the complete prosodic structure assignment algorithm for Spanish. Subsequent comments are keyed to the parenthesized letters.

(A) In the *lexicon,* rhyme segments in roots and derivational affixes may be marked idiosyncratically as extrametrical. This is the formalization of the notion "marked stress." Other rhyme elements are redundantly extrametrical: the predictable extrametricality of consonants outside the derivational stem (e.g., in the terminal element *-is* of [dos]i̶s̶) is registered by the redundancy rule of Predictable Extrametricality (5.55).

Table 5.1 Prosodic Structure Assignment in Spanish

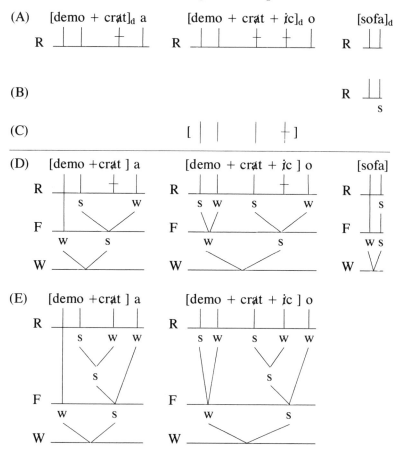

(A)   [demo + crat]$_d$ a   [demo + crat + ic]$_d$ o   [sofa]$_d$

(B)

(C)

(D)   [demo +crat] a   [demo + crat + ic] o   [sofa]

(E)   [demo +crat] a   [demo + crat + ic] o

(F)   *demócrata*   *dèmocrático*   *sofá*

(B) The language-particular prosodic *Strong Foot Rule* (5.64) applies to lexical entries.

(C) Universal *well-formedness conditions* apply wherever possible, in particular in the lexicon, to constrain and/or adjust representations. The universal Peripherality Condition (5.31) is illustrated here: the mark of extrametricality on the rhyme *a* of *crat* is erased in the derivational stem [demo + crặt + ịc] shown in (5.67) since this rhyme is not peripheral in its constituent.

(5.67) [demo + crặt + ịc]

   | | +   +

(D) *Prosodic trees* are constructed on lexical entries adjusted by language-particular rules and universal conditions. Trees are built according to these rules:

a. *Foot level.* Subject to the Branching Condition (5.44), rhymes are gathered into (binary) feet labeled *s* (*w*), proceeding from right to left.[16]

\\/

Unpaired feet (e.g., the first syllable of *demócrata, sofá*) are labeled at the word level.

b. *Word level.* Feet are gathered into (binary) units labeled (*w*) *s*.

(E) *Stray rhymes* are incorporated into prosodic structure by the universal principle of Stray Rhyme Adjunction (5.13). The "structure-preserving" property of this principle has the result that the initial rhyme of *demócrata* cannot be adjoined to the following foot since this would create the illicit foot configuration (5.68).

(5.68) *w s

   \\/

Thus, this rhyme joins the tree at word level, where it does not violate the (*w, s*) labeling of word trees.

(F) For quick reference, the prosodic structure assigned by the foregoing steps is given an approximate translation in segmental terms.

Very little of the procedure just outlined must be stipulated in the grammar of Spanish. In addition to what has already been said in this regard, I note that at step (D) only the labelings (*s, w*) and (*w, s*) need be stipulated at the foot and word levels, respectively. The rest follows from prosodic theory as presented in the recent literature, especially Hayes (1980). This account thus contrasts in a striking way with all previous analyses of Spanish stress, which employ an array of diacritics and other devices on which universal constraints are largely unknown and probably nonexistent.

The present description differs from previous ones also in that, by and large, it automatically accounts for less-than-primary stresses with the same mechanisms used for the assignment of main word stress. I have left some vagueness and inconsistency, however, in the analysis of weaker stresses, which must remain unsatisfactory until better data and/or better understanding of the available data is attained. I add this observation, however: the Branching Condition apparently does not hold in feet dominated by weak branches of the word tree. For example:

(5.69) a.   [àristocrátic]o   *vs.*   b.   *[árist]o

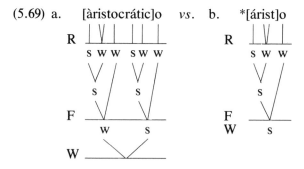

The first foot of *àristo-crático* is certainly well formed, although the identical structure cannot bear primary stress, as shown by hypothetical ill-formed *áristo,* whose ill-formedness results from its violation of the Branching Condition. In theoretical terms, this means that dominant (strong) feet in Spanish are "quantity sensitive" while recessive (weak) feet are "quantity insensitive" (Hayes (1980, chapter 3)).

5.3.2 The Prosodic Cycle: Further Details

Sections 4.3 and 5.1 have presented evidence that prosodic structure trees are constructed cyclically in Spanish. This evidence is consistent with results obtained in part I, where it is shown that prosodic structure construction at the lowest level—that of the syllable—is cyclic also. The cyclic domain for all prosodic levels is the "word." Pretheoretically, prosodic words are identified as the smallest units that can normally constitute isolated utterances; they are identified formally as the constituents bounded by $[\dots]_\alpha$, where α ranges over the category symbols for Noun, Adjective, and Adverb (at the zero-bar level in an X-bar theory). I will now examine certain aspects of the prosodic cycle in three cases: noun and adjective plurals, productively formed diminutives, and productively formed adverbs.

The simplest case of plural formation in nouns and adjectives is that of words with a terminal element, for example $[(\text{loc} + \text{ur})_n\ \text{a}]_N$, whose plural is $[[(\text{loc} + \text{ur})_n\ \text{a}]_N\ \text{s}]_N$.[17] Given that $[\dots]_N$ is a cyclic domain, we expect two cycles of prosodic structure construction in the configuration $[[\dots]_N\ \dots]_N$. However, when no relevant segmental material is added in the second cycle, as in the case at hand, this cycle is vacuous. More specifically, in accordance with the rules and principles specified above, the output of the inner cycle is this:

(5.70) $[\text{loc} + \text{ur} + \text{a}]_N$

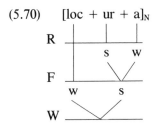

The outer cycle looks like this:

(5.71) $[\text{loc} + \text{úr} + \text{a} + \text{s}]_N$ $\rightarrow$ $[\text{loc} + \text{úr} + \text{a} + \text{s}]_N$

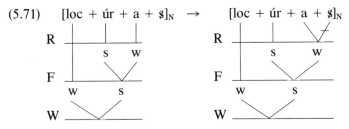

The initial representation is identical to the output of the first cycle, plus the plural morpheme -s (extrametrical in accordance with the rule of Predictable Extrametricality). This segment is incorporated into prosodic structure by the rules of syllable structure, which automatically (re)apply when new segmental material becomes available from any source (and when segments are deleted). Prosodic structure is not otherwise altered in this cycle, nor can it be. In particular, reapplication of foot- and word-tree construction rules triggered by the new [...]$_N$ domain is vacuous.

Now consider the plurals of words with no terminal element, e.g., *vóz, papél, jóven*, etc., which are slightly more complicated. To be certain of covering everything relevant, I will illustrate the maximally complex case, namely, that of words like *jóven*, whose extrametrical final consonant adds a special detail. The output of the first cycle is as follows:

(5.72)   [jóveɲ]$_A$

R ⎵ \̸/

   s w

F ⎵ \/

W   s

Since *jóven* has no terminal element, the segmental representation of the plural is [[jóveɲ]$_A$ eʂ]$_A$, where the plural allomorph *-es* is determined by morphological conditions involving both the stem and the plural suffix.[18] The second cycle thus includes the following steps:

(5.73)   [jóveɲ + eʂ]$_A$ ──ᵃ→   [jóveɲ + eʂ]$_A$ ──ᵇ→   [jóven + eʂ]$_A$

In step (a), the newly accessible segments of the plural suffix are incorporated into prosodic structure by automatic reapplication of syllable-level rules, as in the case of *locúra + s*. In the process, stem-final *-ɲ* becomes the onset of the syllable *-nes,* but without further consequences. In step (b), the foot- and word-tree rules complete the prosodic structure. I follow here the proposals of Kiparsky (1979), whereby cyclic reapplication of these rules makes the minimal alteration in existing structure that yields a well-formed tree. Step (b) is consistent with these proposals in that (i) the existing *s w* foot structure is preserved, (ii) the new foot structure is of the form $s\!\!\!\bigvee\!\!\!w$ and the new weak

foot-node is technically nonbranching—in accordance with the rules and principles specified in 5.3.1.[19]

I turn now to the productive diminutive suffix -((e)c)ito (masculine)/ -((e)c)ita (feminine). (I will not be concerned here with the allomorphy, which is discussed insightfully in Jaeggli (1980).) Consider the derivation of *madrecita*, the diminutive of *madre* 'mother', whose morphological structure (ignoring inessential details) is evidently [[madre]_N cita]_N:

(5.74) *First cycle:*

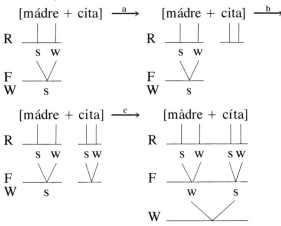

Second cycle:

The first cycle is self-explanatory, as is the initial representation of the second cycle. The changes shown in steps (a), (b), and (c) in the second cycle correspond to the assignment of prosodic structure to the suffixal segments at the level of the syllable, foot, and word, respectively. These changes obviously conform to Kiparsky's requirement of minimum tampering with existing structure. I note only that the downgrading of the strong word-node of *mádre* to weak in step (c) is the prosodic avatar of the SPE cyclic stress reduction convention.

Not all diminutives have such a straightforward derivation. Consider now cases like *pàpelíto,* the diminutive of *papél* 'paper', whose morphological structure is [[papel]ₙ ito]ₙ:

(5.75) *First cycle:*

[papel]ₙ ⟶ [papél]ₙ

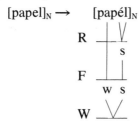

Second cycle:

[papél + ito] —ᵃ'ᵇ→ [papél + ito] —ᶜ→ *[papèl + íto]

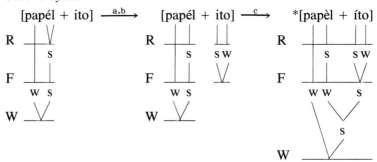

All of the steps in the two cycles are analogous to those of derivation (5.74), yet the final output is wrong; it should be *pàpelíto.* Since the derivation contains no obvious errors, we apparently need a rule of Strong Foot-Label Erasure, which can be stated as follows:

(5.76) *Strong Foot-Label Erasure*

$$s \to \emptyset \ / \underline{\quad} \underset{F}{\overset{}{\boxed{\quad}}} \ s \ w$$

The immediate effect of this rule is to cause the following change in the subrepresentation *papèl-:*

(5.77) papèl- ⟶ papel-

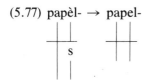

This change automatically sets off the following chain of events:

(5.78)   papel + ito ——ᵃ→   papel + ito ——ᵇ→   pàpel + íto

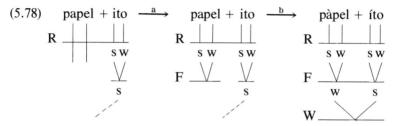

As shown, the tree "mutilated" by the Label Erasure rule is "repaired" without further stipulation by the familiar rules of foot-tree and word-tree construction (steps (a) and (b), respectively).

Another example of the effect of Strong Foot-Label Erasure will also serve as a reminder of an important aspect of cyclic prosodic structure assignment in diminutives.Consider the set *miel* 'honey', diminutive *mielcita*, and *meloso* 'like honey'. The prosodic structure of the first and last words requires little comment:

(5.79) a.   [miél]_N   b.   [(mel + ós)_a o]_A

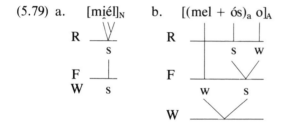

We need observe only that the root morpheme has the diphthong [ie] when stressed but the simple vowel [e] when unstressed, a pattern that appears in hundreds of words. Now note that the same diphthong appears in the diminutive *mielcita*. The prosodic structure of this word, however, is not *mièlcíta but *mĕlcíta*, whose prominence relations are the same as those of *mĕlóso*. Why then does the diphthong appear in the diminutive? Any native speaker will respond that the diminutive is formed from the word *miel*—not the stem *mel-*, as is the related adjective *meloso*. The formal analogue of this intuition is now familiar: the morphological structure of the diminutive is [[miel]_N cita]_N; the output of the first cycle is precisely [miél]_N, where the diphthongal allomorph of the root occurs under stress, as expected. The relevant steps in the second cycle are the following:

(5.80)

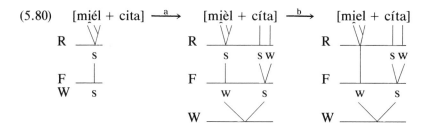

The construction of new prosodic structure at all levels is collapsed into a single step (a). Step (b) then shows the results of Strong Foot-Label Erasure, which yields the correct final representation.[20]

For all its pervasiveness, the monophthong/diphthong alternation illustrated in *meloso/miel* is a lexically restricted phenomenon. (Harris (1977a) provides lengthy discussion.) It is important, then, to see that there are lexically unrestricted processes whose effects, like those of diphthongization, are determined by the cyclic property of prosodic structure construction.[21] Consider the following examples:

(5.81)   *Vowel*   *Glide*

          [melodí + a]$_N$ [melodi̯ + ós + o]$_A$

          [Perú]$_N$ [peru̯ + án + o]$_A$

The words in the right column show the effect of a process of Desyllabification, which applies to unstressed vowels followed by another vowel. (I emphasize that this process has no lexical exceptions.) Now consider words like *grúa* 'crane' and *río* 'river', whose diminutives are *gruíta* (**grui̯ta*) and *riíto* (**ri̯íto*). Desyllabification systematically fails to operate here. Why?[22] The answer becomes clear when we take cyclicity into account. Using the diminutive of *río* for illustration, after the suffix *-ito* has been incorporated into prosodic structure in the second cycle, but before Strong Foot-Label Erasure applies, the representation is this:

(5.82)   [rì + íto]$_N$

Desyllabification cannot apply to the stem vowel because it is stressed. Strong Foot-Label Erasure now applies to produce *ri̊to*, with an unstressed but syllabic segment before the stressed vowel. Desyllabification cannot in turn apply to *ri̊to* because, as a label-changing syllable-level rule, it is intrinsically ordered before Strong Foot-Label Erasure, a label-changing foot-level rule.[23]

The final example is that of adverbs formed with the suffix -*mente*. These adverbs differ from diminutives in that they may contain adjacent stressed sylables; e.g., *formàlménte, èficàzménte* (cf. **papèlíto, *mièlcíta*). Obviously, the rule of Strong Foot-Label Erasure must be prevented from applying to -*mente* adverbs. Recall that phrases may also have adjacent stresses; e.g., *Josè báila, và prónto, mùy mál, ciudàd bélla,* etc. I therefore propose that -*mente* adverbs are exempt from Strong Foot-Label Erasure because (i) this rule applies only within single words, and (ii) -*mente* adverbs are not single words. I suggest that they do not have the structure [[...]$_A$ mente]$_A$ as proposed earlier, but rather [[...]$_A$ [mente]$_C$]$_A$; C is some cyclic category, probably Noun, but its precise identification is not crucial here. This structure captures the generalizations about -*mente* adverbs mentioned earlier—in particular, the fact that they have phrasal stress rather than the prominence relations of single words—but of course it does not explain these generalizations in the strong sense.

The task of formulating a genuinely explanatory account is more than I can undertake here, but perhaps the following facts are appropriately suggestive. As all "first year" students of Spanish must learn, -*mente* is a "separable affix" in the sense that it appears on only the last adverb of a conjoined series; e.g., *Los muchachos trabajaron rápida y eficazmente* 'The boys worked rapidly and effectively'. Feminine singular *rápida* does not agree with masculine plural *muchachos,* as would a normal adjective; it can only be the base with which -*mente* is associated discontinuously. (As mentioned earlier, -*mente* attaches to feminine singular adjectives for historical reasons.) Thus, the structure of the conjunction is evidently not (5.83a) but rather (5.83b):

(5.83)

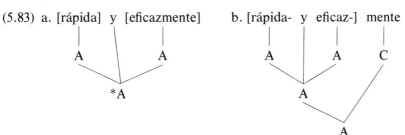

If the structure of the conjunction is $[[...]_A \ [\text{mente}]_C]_A$, then this is presumably the structure of a simple adverb like *eficazmente* as well. Adverbial *-mente* is unique among Spanish suffixes in having quasi-word status. In particular, the diminutive suffix does not have it. For example, although *rápida y eficazmente* is understood as *rápidamente y eficazmente,* it is not possible for *perro y gatito* 'dog and cat (dim.)' to be understood as *perrito y gatito* 'dog (dim.) and cat (dim.)'.

Appendix:
Movable Stresses

Stress normally falls on the "same" syllable in singular/plural pairs:

(A.1)	Singular Stress		V-final Singular	C-final Singular
Final:	Sg.		mamá	azúl
	Pl.		mamás	azúles
Penultimate:	Sg.		abuéla	cadáver
	Pl.		abuélas	cadáveres
Antepenultimate:	Sg.		esdrújulo	hipótesis
	Pl.		esdrújulos	hipótesis

We have seen that the description developed in part II accounts for these data.

Now consider these six exceptional words in which stress shifts to the right in the plural:

(A.2)	Singular	Plural
a.	régimen	regímenes
	espécimen	especímenes
	ínterin	intérines
b.	ómicron	omicrónes
	júnior	junióres
c.	carácter	caractéres

It is *de rigueur* to say something about these exceptional cases in any discussion of Spanish stress.

The stress shift here has been seen as a consequence of the already mentioned general restriction of stress in Spanish to one of the last three syllables of a word. Invocation of this restriction is not a priori unreasonable, but it turns out to have no explanatory force. In the first place, the restriction itself can hardly be the mechanism that "moves" the stress, nor does it specify how far to move it. Contrast *régimen/ regímenes*, where a violation is avoided by moving the stress one syllable to the right, with *ómicron/omicrónes*, where stress moves two syllables. Why move two syllables when a one-syllable jump to **omícrones* would suffice? Furthermore, the "one of the last three syllables" restriction is obviously not even relevant to *carácter/caractéres*, since an "unshifted" plural *carácteres* does not violate the restriction.

These cases are marginal, both in the sense that there are only six of them and also in that only two (*régimen/carácter*) are in general use. It seems evident that the exceptional forms are maintained only by prescriptivist pressure, the source of which is certainly no mystery: one need look no farther than the stress of Latin *caractēr/caractēres*, *júniōr/juniōres*, *régĭmĕn/regĭmĕnes*, etc. This pressure is not totally successful. The regular form *carácteres*, rather than *caractéres*, has long existed as a popular plural of *carácter*. Similarly, popular *interín/ interínes* competes in some dialects with erudite *ínterin/intérines*, as does popular *regímen/regímenes* with erudite *régimen/regímenes*.

It should now be clear why I relegated these cases to an appendix. I believe that the considerations just sketched justify the position that we are confronted with "extragrammatical" forms. That is, speakers probably memorize these forms in isolation from the generalizations internalized on the basis of the rest of the language. If this is what really happens, then we should not modify an otherwise well-motivated linguistic description solely to accommodate these aberrant cases.[1] Still, there may be some interest in trying to determine, at least as an exercise, what adjustments speakers might make in order to bring such accretions into line with their internalized grammars.

In Harris (1973) I (like others before and after me) treated the cases under discussion as a uniform phenomenon. That is, I tried to provide an analysis in which there was a unique peculiarity shared by all cases. This was a mistake. The only reason to suppose that the various cases are all of a kind was that they allegedly obeyed the "stress one of the last three syllables" restriction. But we have seen that this explains nothing. It would therefore be best to set aside only aesthetic compulsions in order to see what the popular forms reveal. Comparison of popular *carácter/carácteres* (versus erudite *caractéres*) with abundant regular pairs like *cadáver/cadáveres*, *ángel/ángeles*, *cráter/cráteres*, etc., suggests that plural *caractéres* is anomalous while singular *ca-*

rácter is normal. The case of *interín/intérines* is different. Here the popular version is *interín/interínes*, just like regular *bailarín/bailarínes*, *boletín/boletínes*, *calcetín/calcetínes*, *gachupín/gachupínes*, *mandarín/mandarínes*, *paladín/paladínes*, etc. This suggests that in erudite *ínterin/intérines* both singular and plural are odd. The popular version of erudite *régimen/regímenes* is *regímen/regímenes*, which of course finds its analogue in standard (and regular) *exámen/exámenes*, *abdómen/abdómenes*, *certámen/certámenes*, *volúmen/volúmenes*, etc. These suggest that singular *régimen* is anomalous while plural *regímenes* is normal.

In short, there is nothing of interest to say about singular *carácter* or plural *regímenes*, whose prosodic structure is assigned to the representations [caracteŗ], [[regimeɲ]eṣ] by the rules and principles given in section 5.3. The cases we must cope with—if we wish to pursue the exercise—are plural *caractéres*, singular *régimen*, and the pair *ínterin/intérines*.

What representation minimally different from [[caracteŗ]eṣ] will result in *caractéres*? The answer is provided by many regular singular/plural pairs like *alfilér(es)*, *alquilér(es)*, *anochecér(es)*, *bachillér(es)*, *cancillér(es)*, *amanecér(es)*, *mercadér(es)*, *quehacér(es)*, etc., namely, [[caracter]eṣ], where stem-final *r* is not extrametrical. The derivational steps of interest are the following:

(A.3) [caractér] → [caractér]eṣ → [caractér]eṣ

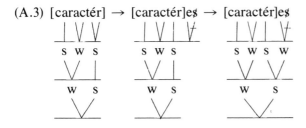

The first representation is the output of the first cycle, in which, in particular, the final rhyme of the inflectional stem is dominated by a strong foot-node because this rhyme branches. The second representation shows the result of syllable structure adjustment in the second cycle. In the final representation the newly formed rhyme is linked to the tree with minimal disturbance of existing structure. In short, the oddity of plural *caractéres* vis-à-vis singular *carácter* is that stem-final *r* is not extrametrical in the plural.

Similarly, the representation minimally different from [regimeɲ] that could be assigned the prosodic structure of *régimen* would seem to be [regímeɲ]. But [regímeɲ] would be adjusted immediately to [regimeɲ] by the Peripherality Condition. We do not want a lexical representation, even an irregular one, that is at odds with a presumably universal well-formedness condition. The representation [[regí]meɲ] avoids the problem (although it is otherwise unmotivated). That is, [regí] is a sort of derivational stem nested within a derivational stem.[2] Prosodic structure can be assigned to this ad hoc but viable representation as follows:

(A.4)   [[regí]meɲ]   →   [[regí]meɲ]

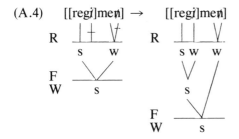

(The arrow represents the operation of Stray Rhyme Adjunction.) *Espécimen/especímenes* is obviously amenable to the same treatment, as is *ínterin/intérines* if we postulate for the singular the structure (A.5a) and for the plural (A.5b), like [[regimeɲ]eʂ].

(A.5) a. [[intɘr]iɲ]   b. [[interiɲ]es]

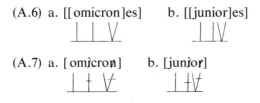

The morpheme *inter-* can easily be identified as the familiar one found in *interino, intermedio*, etc.

The most recalcitrant cases are *ómicron, júnior*. Prosodic structure can be readily assigned to the plurals *omicrónes, junióres* via the representations (A.6a,b). The singulars, however, demand something like (A.7a,b).

(A.6) a. [[omicron]es]   b. [[junior]es]

(A.7) a. [omícroɲ]   b. [juníoɾ]

These present two problems. First, they violate the Peripherality Condition. Second, they cannot be further bracketed in any plausible way so as to circumvent it. For example, etymological *o* + *micron* is no help, and it is not accessible to the native speaker in any event. There is no alternative to [[omí]croɲ] or [[omícr]oɲ] and [[juní]oɾ], which will give the desired outputs although they are totally unmotivated.

I conclude this exercise with the summary observation that the more common of the deviant words under discussion (*caractéres*, *régimen*) can be assimilated to the normal patterns by means of relatively minor adjustments in their lexical representation. The more exotic examples (*ómicron*, *júnior*) require more radical, less rational alterations in their lexical entries.[3]

Notes

Introduction

1. Among the most important recent works in this line of investigation are Halle and Vergnaud (1980, in preparation), Kiparsky (1979), Liberman and Prince (1977), McCarthy (1979a,b), Safir (1979), and Selkirk (1978, 1980, in preparation).

2. Bell and Hooper (1978) cite much interesting evidence supporting this view.

3. Though I do not know who first advanced this argument, it has been a fairly prominent feature, implicitly or explicitly, in recent studies of syllable structure.

4. If this argument is correct, then the "linear" approach of Hooper (1976)— like its predecessor Hooper (1972), which also treats syllables as strings of segments bounded by the special symbol $—does not provide an adequate characterization of syllable organization. Current investigation suggests that morphological and syntactic boundary symbols such as "+", "#", etc., have the same status as symbols that mark the boundaries of syllables. That is, it seems likely that rules refer directly to hierarchical aspects of morphological and syntactic organization rather than to special boundary symbols. Some of the discussion and most of the references in section 3.6 are relevant to this issue.

Chapter 1

1. The monosyllabicity of *buey* is represented in (1.1) by associating all of its segments with a single branching tree rooted in the node σ, for "syllable." I transcribe the nonsyllabic counterparts of [u i] as [u̯ i̯], a distinction not consistently represented in the standard orthography.

Only the first representation in (1.1) is countenanced by theories of syllable structure of the type presented in Kahn (1976), which characterize syllables as tree structures in which segments do not form intermediate-level constituents. The existence of syllable-internal constituents larger than segments is also denied by theories in which syllables are represented as $-bounded strings, e.g.,

Hooper (1972, 1976). Thus, any evidence that supports subsyllabic groupings of segments is counterevidence to both theories like Kahn's and theories like Hooper's. (The two are apparently not simply notational variants, however, since the former but not the latter permits "ambisyllabic" segments.)

2. Unfortunately, they do not provide any independent argument that the grammar selected by their evaluation metric is the correct one. However, the authors were not unaware of or uninterested in the problem; cf. Contreras and Saporta (1960).

3. In present tense second person plural verb forms, the final syllable may contain six segments, e.g., *a-griais* (indicative), *a-grieis* (subjunctive). I will show below that these forms, which are restricted to certain dialects in any event, are not genuine exceptions to the five-segment restriction. The grammars of both Saporta and Contreras (1962) and Hooper (1976) generate six-segment syllables freely, ignoring their special status.

4. It is a separate question whether or not there is any motivation for recognizing the nucleus and coda as constituents once the subsuming constituent is recognized. I will argue later that such motivation does not exist in Spanish.

   Incidentally, the template of Hooper (1976, chapter 11), in which syllable-internal constituents play no role, correctly characterizes syllables of the type (1.7a) as ill formed. However, the same template characterizes other ill-formed syllable types as permissible (e.g., **praim-po*, **[ñuiux]-to*) and certain well-formed types as impermissible (e.g., *pers-picaz*). The rather accidental nature of the predictions of Hooper's account makes discussion difficult.

5. The qualification "as nouns and adjectives" responds to the fact that words like *estú-dia-lo, lím-pie-se,* etc., are well formed. They are not nouns or adjectives, however, but rather verb forms (*estúdia, límpie*) followed by clitic pronouns (*lo, se*). Such sequences are written as a single word in the standard orthography, but in fact clitics are "stress neutral," that is, they fall outside the domain of stress rules and thus do not affect the stress of words to which they are cliticized. By the same token, a word such as *hagá-mos-lo,* which consists of the verb form *hagámos* plus the clitic *lo,* is not an exception to the generalization illustrated in (1.10), despite the closed penult. Further discussion of the need to view stress rules in Spanish as conditions of well-formedness in particular morphological domains rather than as direct limitations on pronunciation appears in chapter 2.

6. With innocuous oversimplification, we may take the segmental inventory of Spanish to be as follows (parenthesized segments do not occur in all dialects):

Consonantal				*Nonconsonantal*			
				Syllabic		*Nonsyllabic*	
p	t	č	k	i	u	i̯	u̯
b	d	(ɟ)	g	e	o		
f	s	(ž)	x	a			
m	n	ñ					
l	(ʎ)						
r							

A word about dialects and informants: In general, I will ignore Iberian dialects here (hence the absence of [Θ] just above). Among the (almost exclusively Latin American) native speakers I have consulted, Mexicans predominate by a considerable margin. Still, the reasonable convergence of judgments indicates that this study probably comes fairly close to being pan-dialectal. A few clearly dialect-particular phenomena will be pointed out, however.

7. Flap [r] is replaced by a trill word initially and under certain conditions elsewhere. Palatal [ñ] occurs freely in internal position but is rare initially. Dictionaries generally list only *ñapa, ñato, ñoño, ñu,* and maybe one or two others, as opposed to hundreds of words with internal *ñ*.

8. Not all dialects have word-initial *tl*. Those that have it also allow *tl* as an internal onset. Of the dialects without initial *tl,* some allow *tl* as an internal onset while others require heterosyllabic *t-l*. I know of no word with [xr] other than the loan *Jruschef*.

9. I ignore a few Mexican volcanoes like *Citlaltépetl, Popocatépetl,* and *Iztaccíhuatl,* which may be pronounced with a final syllabic *l*. These and other indigenous toponyms are easily tagged as unassimilated loans.

10. This is not to deny that the lexicon of contemporary dialects of Spanish contains words like *istmo, erg, marxismo, parking, living,* etc., in which the indicated rhyme clusters may be pronounced essentially as suggested by the spelling (by some speakers on some occasions, at the very least). The existence of such words merely underscores the importance of attempting to understand native judgments of well-formedness, as opposed to mechanically describing a corpus. In this regard, see Chomsky's remarks on the distinction between "grammar" and "language" as the object of linguistic inquiry in Chomsky (1980, especially chapter 3) and Chomsky (1981, especially 7ff).

11. Some of the sequences in (1.21) are statistically infrequent (e.g., *eu, ou*), but all are readily pronounceable, could be used in nonce forms, etc. Unstressed *iu* and *iu* seem to be fairly freely interchangeable.

12. In making this tally I disregarded everything whose legitimacy might be questioned, e.g., acronyms and all proper names (even the name of the newspaper itself, *Excelsior*). I also disregarded inflections, the prepositions *con, sin, por,* the article *el,* and a few other items that would inflate the count of rhymes with sonorant consonants.

13. I have raised this issue primarily because misleading statements have appeared in the literature concerning the status of obstruents in rhymes. For example, Hooper (1976) claims that "although other obstruents besides /s/ appear orthographically in syllable-final position, in casual speech such C's are systematically omitted" (p. 195, note 1). Although there do exist "consonant-weak" dialects that have processes of consonant reduction and deletion, Hooper overstates the case for these dialects and misrepresents "consonant-strong" dialects, in which there is no systematic deletion of obstruents in any position in any style of speech. The consonants in question in this section are all real, "pronounced" segments.

Chapter 2

1. I take this to be an interesting empirical hypothesis that should be abandoned only if it is shown to be necessary to retreat to the weaker position that branching is n-ary, $n > 2$. I am not aware that evidence to this effect is available. (We saw in section 1.1 that Saporta and Contreras's claim for ternary branching in Spanish syllables is empirically disproven.) Furthermore, binary branching in prosodic structure neatly houses the binary strong/weak relation which appears to play a central role in prosodic structure (cf. Liberman and Prince (1977), Kiparsky (1979), etc.).

2. I include [+consonantal] in these representations solely to indicate the conditions that the terminal string must meet; [+consonantal] is not a node label. The only node labels we have recognized in syllable structure representation are σ, O, and R.

3. Kaye and Lowenstamm (1979) argue, in effect, that in the unmarked case the maximum number of segments in the rhymes of a language L is at least one greater than the maximum number of segments in the onsets of L. Spanish of course has this property. However, the length restriction under discussion would follow as a consequence only from the stronger statement that the maximum length of rhymes is exactly one segment greater than that of onsets. Kaye and Lowenstamm do not argue for this stronger statement, and numerous counterexamples to it seem to exist.

4. The notion of prosodic skeleton is developed in Halle and Vergnaud (1980) and McCarthy (1979a); it is put to crucial use in a classical problem of Spanish phonology in Harris (1980b).

5. I follow here the general principle of tree structure whereby nonbranching (ia) is equivalent to, and automatically adjusted to, (ib):

(i) a. X   b. X

Thus, the structure of (2.11a) is shown as (iia) rather than as (iib).

(ii) a. G V   b. G V

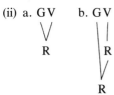

6. I enclose the phoneme /s/ in diagonals in order to avoid confusion with the relational mark s(trong).

7. Notice that onsets must be formed before rhymes (here and in general). Otherwise, there is no principled way to prevent the incorrect syllabification (i).

(i) (e)sfera

RR

No language-particular stipulation to this effect is required in Spanish, however, since the empirically correct application of our syllable structure rules follows from the "simplicity" condition of Kiparsky (1979), whereby (in particular) (iia) is to be preferred over (iib).

(ii) a. ...e r a   b. ...e r φa

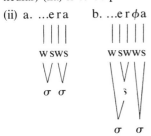

8. The specification of *r* as [+continuant] and *l* as [−continuant] is justified by the following generalization: *b*, *d*, *g* are realized as continuant β, ð, ɣ after continuants and as noncontinuants after (homorganic) noncontinuants, e.g., *frau*[ð]*e* vs. *gran*[d]*e*. Now notice the same pattern in *cer*[ð]*a* vs. *ce̲l*[d]*a*.

9. The generalization expressed in these two filters collapses if we consider *d* as [+continuant], that is, if we take into account its continuant allophone ð. Evidently, then, (a) filters apply to underlying representations, and (b) stops underlie the alternations *b*/β, *d*/ð, and *g*/ɣ. However, Lozano (1979) argues that evidence allegedly supporting basic stops in these alternations is inconclusive. Lozano's arguments on this point are carefully constructed and completely convincing, in my opinion. She argues further that the segments underlying the alternating pairs are neither the stop nor the fricative members, but rather abstract segments not specified for continuancy. It is the latter claim that seems to be incompatible with the generalization expressed in the filters proposed here. I believe that a "best of all possible worlds" position is available—that is, an account in which Lozano's claims and the filters are both valid—but further discussion would take us too far afield.

10. I will not deal here with the fact that the lax nonstrident palatal continuant [ʝ] does not cluster, in the dialects in which this segment occurs. The historical reason for this is clear: [ʝ] derives diachronically from the glide [i̯] and the liquid [ʎ], neither of which can appear in two-segment onsets since they are not obstruents. In most dialects, there is no synchronic reason to derive [ʝ] from /ʎ/, but there is evidence for deriving it from /i̯/, at least in some cases. I will return to [ž] ~ [i̯] alternations in section 3.4, but will leave many questions involving [ʝ] unresolved.

11. It is clear from the history of Spanish that all instances of modern [x] in patrimonial words come from sources that preclude its being followed by a liquid. Native *ojo* = [oxo] 'eye' provides an example. The etymon is Proto-

Romance *oklo,* which underwent a series of changes that includes the following steps: $kl \rightarrow gl \rightarrow yl \rightarrow y\Lambda \rightarrow \Lambda \rightarrow \check{z} \rightarrow \check{s} \rightarrow x$. Since [x] derives from a cluster ending in *l,* and since there were no *kll* clusters, [x] cannot be followed by another *l.*

12. The vowel clusters in cases like *moho* [móo], *golpeé* [golpeé] are hetero-morphic: *moh* + *o* ('mold' plus class marker), *golpe* + *é* ('hit', first person sin-gular preterit). Clusters of identical vowels within a morpheme are rare and tend to simplify to single vowels. For example, *Saavedra, alcohol* may be pro-nounced *S*[aa]*védra, alc*[oó]*l;* but *S*[a]*védra, alc*[ó]*l* are more natural and do not smack of hyperprecise spelling pronunciations. All of the cases mentioned here should be analyzed as disyllabic. There is thus no systematic minimal contrast betwen long and short vowels in Spanish.

13. There is a partial correlation between terminal element and gender. More often than not, words with *-o* are masculine and words with *-a* are feminine; otherwise, the relationship is random. Additional discussion of terminal ele-ments and related morphological matters appears below and in part II.

14. This was suggested by an anonymous MIT Press reader, to whom I am indebted for a number of extremely valuable criticisms of an earlier version of this monograph.

15. Selkirk (1978, in preparation) discusses at length the lack of isomorphism between prosodic structure and syntactic structure. Additional material on this topic from Spanish appears in the next section.

Chapter 3

1. For example, at the Simposio de Dialectología del Caribe Hispánico (Cara-cas, Venezuela, 4–6 June 1980), five out of nine phonology papers had aspira-tion as their primary or sole topic.

2. *Nosotros* may be pronounced *no*[h]*otros,* which suggests that it contains an internal word boundary: *nos # otros.* This is hardly surprising in view of the independent existence of both *nos* and *otros* (cf. French *nous autres*). *Entonces* may be pronounced [ẽtõhe], which is not so easy to deal with. Note that (3.2b) does not account for it either.

3. Cibaeño is the dialect of Spanish spoken in El Cibao, a north central region of the Dominican Republic. I am indebted directly to Guitart (1980b) and indi-rectly to Golibart (1976) and Alba (1979) for the data in this section.

4. Liquids are also sometimes deleted entirely in Cibaeño, but I will not pursue this question since it is neutral with respect to the theoretical point of this sec-tion. The references cited in the previous note contain extensive discussion of Cibaeño liquid deletion.

5. This is an oversimplification, but an innocuous one in the present context. I will examine the domain of syllabification more carefully in the next section. Discussion of the domain of stress assignment rules will be found in part II.

As (3.11) suggests, the syntactic notion "left sister" probably plays a role in the specification of prosodic words—the article *el* is a left sister of *aviso*, but the pronoun *él* is not a left sister of *avisa*—but I cannot pursue this here.

6. The quotation marks are in recognition of Kiparsky (1979).

7. I have altered Contreras's rule to the extent of substituting a phonetically uninterpreted symbol *L* for his *l̄* = [ʎ], a palatal lateral, as the input to (3.14). I make this substitution in order to sidestep controversy concerning the underlying representation of the segment *L*, which is irrelevant to present concerns. This controversy arises from the fact that *L*, i.e., orthographic *ll*, is realized as the palatal lateral [ʎ] in some dialects but as a range of nonlateral palatals in other dialects, a range that overlaps the realizations of other phonemes. This issue is irrelevant here because all dialects depalatalize under exactly the same circumstances, regardless of how they happen to realize *L* in nondepalatalizing environments (or other phonemes in any environment).

8. It is in relevant respects the same structure postulated by Contreras. He writes *doncel # es*, for example, using a boundary symbol instead of labeled brackets; the internal # provides the environment for the operation of (3.14) in this case. Harris (1980b) contains discussion of the plural allomorphy *-es* ~ *-s*, as in *donceles, doncellas*. The examples under discussion are in no way special in this respect.

9. This proposal is supported by the fact that stress rules also cycle on the same morphological constituent, as we will see in part II. These comments on cyclicity serve only as a placeholder; I return to the topic in section 3.5.

10. Nasal Depalatalization as illustrated here is a special case of a more general process, common to all dialects, whereby all nasals—not just *ñ*—are neutralized in syllable rhymes. I illustrate only the special case of *ñ* → *n* here in order to facilitate comparison with Contreras (1977). Further discussion of the general neutralization process appears in Harris (forthcoming).

11. An exhaustive list of references would be far too long. I therefore fall back on a common criterion of selection, namely, I cite my own works: Harris (1969, 1972, 1973, 1977a, 1980a, and ms.).

12. Markedness can be implicated in these data in another way as well: not only is V-CV unmarked with respect to VC-V, but also obstruents are "better" [−syllabic] segments than glides in syllable-initial position. Rule (3.36) is Porteño's way of enforcing observance of the latter markedness principle.

13. In some Puerto Rican dialects [r] is replaced by a lateral [l̆] in rhymes and [r̄] is replaced by a velar fricative [x̂]—I use ad hoc symbols in order to avoid commitment regarding the exact quality of these segments. In this case, *salir rápido*, for example, could conceivably be pronounced *sali*[l̆x̂]*ápido*, distinct from *salí rápido* = *salí*[x̂]*ápido*. I tend to doubt that such a distinction is possible, but I do not know the facts.

14. There is almost no dialect variation on this point, and very little variation in fine phonetic detail within a given dialect (e.g., some assibilation of *r* of *tr*

clusters in some dialects). Singers occasionally trill the *r* in Cr onsets for stylistic effect, but this is no more representative of normal speech than the trilling of *r*s in song by English speakers. In Spanish, not surprisingly, singers never substitute a trill for [r] in the one position of contrast, i.e., between vowels.

15. The stem of *honra* appears also in *honrado, honradez, honrar, honrador, honroso,* etc., and that of *honor* in *honorar, honorable, honorario, honorífico,* etc. The two sets of derived words are not coextensive: **honoradez, *honrífico,* etc.

16. I belabor the point because this phenomenon has been confused with the behavior of Spirantization, which is different. Spirantized phones do occur in word-initial utterance-medial position (e.g., *la gata = la* [ɣ]*ata*), although [r] is impossible in this environment.

17. The most common meaning of *roer* is 'to gnaw (with the teeth)', but it is also used in the sense of *El agua roe la piedra* 'Water eats away/erodes rock'.

18. Mario Montalbetti reports an extremely popular kind of language play in his dialect of Lima, Peru, which involves metathesis of syllables; e.g., normal [r̄]*aya* becomes *ya*[r]*a,* not **ya*[r̄]*a.* That is, the segment which surfaces as [r] in metathesized *ya*[r]*a* must be realized as [r̄] in word-initial position in the normal unmetathesized word. This example suggests with great force that (3.46) expresses an "active" alternation.

19. In his description of "R.P." Castilian, Navarro Tomás (1965) mentions a range from a weakly articulated fricative to a long trill, in free or stylistic variation. There is also much variation between dialects.

20. Actually, [r-ñ] is also missing. However, since *ñ* does not cluster with any consonant, the absence of *rñ* is expected rather than exceptional.

21. A methodological note: Some linguists are suspicious of arguments involving gaps, such as the one in Chomsky and Halle (1968, 191ff) that leads to the conclusion that the underlying vowel of English *boy, coin,* etc., is the tense low front rounded vowel /ɔ̄/. The argument involving the gap in (3.54) differs in several important ways, one being that it does not lead to the postulation of a new underlying segment or new rules.

22. Untrained native speakers can also identify the source of the deviance quite readily and without prompting. A typical reaction: "La peor [de *cámarra, cámacha, cámaña, cámata*] es *cámarra,* porque el acento está dislocado. Pienso en *cigárra, chamárra, chatárra, amárra . . .*" 'The worst one [...] is *cámarra,* because the stress is out of place. I think of *cigárra* [...]'. For the nonnative speaker I should point out that *cámarra, cámacha, cámaña, cámata* are nonexistent words that I made up in order to elicit native judgments; *cigárra, chamárra, chatárra, amárra* are all real (well-formed) words offered spontaneously by the informant.

23. García-Bellido (1979) takes syllables into account, but her work is hampered by an insufficiently general view.

24. The syllable structure shown here is crucial. The preceding representation, in which [r̄] is still a rhyme, should not be considered ill formed. It reflects a pronunciation hyperprecise enough to prevent resyllabification. Such a pronunciation is possible, though outside the colloquial norm.

25. As we shall see in chapter 4, the same is true of the rules of stress assignment, which I claim are also cyclic. In that chapter I will show in considerable detail how stress assignment is dependent on prior assignment of syllable structure.

26. One might think of postulating a postcyclic "antiaspiration" rule that would turn the incorrect [h] of *me[h]e[h] (and all analogous cases) back to [s]. Such a move, however, would be not only inelegant but also impossible. This is illustrated by representations like the following, which show that [h] in word-final position remains [h] after syllable structure is adjusted over word boundaries:

(i) a. el me[h] entero   b. me[s]e[h] entero[h]

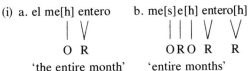

      O R   O R O R   R

  'the entire month'   'entire months'

27. This is the judgment of Tracy D. Terrell, the leading investigator of the phenomenon. (See Terrell (1975, 1978a, 1979).) I am indebted to Prof. Terrell for patient discussion of the dialectological data. It should not be inferred, however, that he endorses the theoretical orientation of this monograph.

28. It is not the case that [...]$_{X^0}$ is the *only* cyclic domain permitted in *any* version of Lexical Phonology. Richer versions than the one suggested by (3.67) might allow additional presyntactic loops, say, between levels of morphological rules. Postlexical cycles, however, would not fall within the leading assumptions of Lexical Phonology. (Note in this regard that (3.67) predicts the result of Liberman and Prince (1977) that phrase-level stress assignment in English is not cyclic.)

29. As we shall see in part II, the same is true of stress assignment rules in Spanish, which build (arboreal) prosodic structure rather than changing features.

30. Other properties are not shared by Aspiration and Velarization. Aspiration is clearly neutralizing in one set of dialects and evidently obligatory in another, overlapping, set. Velarization, on the other hand, is evidently obligatory in some dialects but neutralizing in none. There is no motivation for postulating underlying /ŋ/ in any dialect.

31. The rules listed in (3.74) are all related in one way or another, directly or indirectly, to syllable structure. This is no doubt due to the fact that this monograph focuses precisely on syllable structure.

Chapter 4

1. For example, Clements and Ford (1979), Goldsmith (1976a,b), Halle and Vergnaud (1980, in preparation), Kiparsky (1979), Liberman (1975), McCarthy (1979b), Safir (1979), Selkirk (1978, 1980), Vergnaud (1979). In the following discussion I assume some familiarity with this line of investigation.

2. In contrast, no such constraint applies across word divisions, e.g., reál àcadémia, Fidél Cástro.

3. Data on nonprimary stresses in Spanish are not easy to come by. Collections of primary observations do not usually record prosodic information other than location of primary word stress. There are a few exceptions, of which the most detailed and reliable is probably Stockwell, Bowen, and Silva-Fuenzalida (1956). Nor surprisingly, the generative literature on nonprimary stresses in Spanish is meager.

4. Diphthongs appear as predicted in -mente adverbs, e.g., fuèrteménte 'strongly'. Suñer (1975) discusses in generative terms the phrasal character of stress in these forms (note especially the adjacent stresses in formàlménte, prohibited in ordinary words, as observed in section 4.2.5). The prosodic properties of diminutives are further exemplified and discussed in Harris (1974).

5. Continuing the practice of part I, in cases of potential confusion I transcribe the nonsyllabic counterparts of [i u] as [i̯ u̯], a distinction not made consistently in the standard orthography.

6. It is demonstrated in section 1.1 that prenuclear glides are members of the rhyme rather than of the syllable onset, and also that the branching of onsets in the penult does not affect the possibility of antepenultimate stress.

7. We should not lose sight of the general point that existing analyses of Spanish stress—including of course my own—are not just observationally inadequate, but descriptively incorrect as well. This follows from the fact that they cannot incorporate the new data of section 4.4 without modifications so radical that there would be no sense in calling them "the same" analyses. Obviously, no theoretical conclusions can be drawn from descriptively incorrect grammars. Therefore, all theoretical claims based on existing descriptions of Spanish stress—for example, the alleged superiority of "concrete" over "abstract" analyses claimed by some—are entirely without force.

Chapter 5

1. Cf. section 3.3 and following sections, where the same morphological structures (and the same notational devices) are seen to play a role in syllable structure and related phenomena of segmental phonology. The claim that adverbs have the same set of terminal elements as nouns and adjectives is radically novel, but I believe that its correctness is scarcely in doubt.

   Spanish nouns have lexically fixed gender (masculine or feminine); adjectives display gender agreement with nouns (masculine and feminine forms may or may not be distinct). Nouns and adjectives are inflected for number; e.g., $[[(sed)_n \ a]_N \ s]_N$ 'silks', $[[(alert)_a \ a]_A \ s]_A$ 'alert (plural)', etc. Adverbs are invariable; that is, they do not have gender and are not inflected for number.

2. Examples like *bueno/bondad, bello/beldad* 'beautiful'/'beauty', etc., where the suffix is consonant-initial, show that these cases illustrate a genuine morphological phenomenon, not simply the effect of a commonly found phonological rule $V \rightarrow \emptyset \ / \ \_\_\_ \ V$.

3. In chapter 3, especially sections 3.3 and 3.6, I argue on quite independent grounds that syllable structure assignment also cycles at the level of the word. Other properties of this constituent are discussed in Harris (1977c).

4. See Hayes (1979, 1980) for extended discussion of the motivation behind this concept, as well as the convention of Stray Rhyme Adjunction to be introduced immediately below in the text.

5. As extrametricality is investigated in more and more languages, it might turn out that the Peripherality Condition is too strong. It would not be surprising to find a language that was like Spanish in relevant respects except that instead of sets of words like *número/numérico/numeróso* and *ídolo/idólatra/idolatría*, it would contain sets like *número/númerico/numeróso* and *ídolo/ídolatra/idolatría*. This would mean that uninterrupted sequences of extrametrical segments are allowed as long as the entire sequence is peripheral (e.g., (i)),

(i) [númer + ic]o

while nonperipheral extrametrical segments separated from a constituent edge by a nonextrametrical segment are still excluded (e.g., (ii)).

(ii) *[númer + os]o

In this case, the universal Peripherality Condition would have to be replaced by a weaker universal *Discontinuity Prohibition* of the form (iii), where *b* is not extrametrical.

(iii) $a \rightarrow a \ / \ [X \ \_\_\_ \ Y \ b \ Z]$

The actual facts of Spanish would then require an additional language-particular rule of *Extrametricality Annulment* of the form (iv),

(iv) $a \rightarrow a \ / \ [X \ \_\_\_ \ Y \ b \ Z]$

which prohibits sequences of extrametrical elements within the derivational stem. Naturally, we will prefer the stronger Peripherality Condition stated in the main text until it is shown to be necessary to weaken it.

6. *Régimen* will be discussed further in the appendix. There are six other words like it, all of them uncommon, which I now list in more or less increasing order

of exoticness: *espécimen, ínterin, Júpiter, ómicron, asíndeton, bustrófedon.*
The existence of the last two is undreamed of by the nonspecialist. I have
ranked *Júpiter* as relatively outlandish because no one knows what the plural is
(*Júpiters?, Jupíteres?, Jupitéres?*), while everybody knows that the plural of
régimen is *regímenes*, with displacement of primary stress to the right.

7. Part I of this monograph provides such an account. Incidentally, languages
in which the structure (or even the presence) of the syllable onset is relevant for
stress rules seem to be rare or nonexistent.

8. Hayes (1980, especially section 3.3) provides the theoretical context into
which the Branching Condition fits.

9. I cannot pursue the point here, but the representation *Venezuẹla,* and all
others that share the relevant property, should probably be ruled out by the
general theory in any event. In the rhyme *uẹ, e* is the strong element, which
should not be able to be marked extrametrical. (Recall that Stray Rhyme Adjunction connects stray elements as recessive branches of the nearest available
node.)

10. The Branching Condition predicts that (i) should be impossible.

(i) alícuota

     \/   .

Perhaps here and also in the exceptional case of *ventrílocuo* (mentioned in section 5.2.2) we are dealing with the rounded velar segment k^w rather than the
sequence *ku*. There is independent, but rather weak, evidence for rounded velars in Spanish. I will not pursue it, though, since only two troublesome forms
are involved, one of which (*alícuota*) the overwhelming majority of speakers
have never encountered.

11. Cf. **toráx + ico* but *léx + ico, tóx + ico* and **toráct + ico* but *sin-
táct + ico, didáct + ico.* A unified description of these and other relevant data
is given in Harris (1980b).

12. The role of the variable Z in the environment of this rule will be illustrated,
in part, directly below. Full illustration would require discussion of verb stress,
which I have not presented. The following examples of verb forms are suggestive, however:

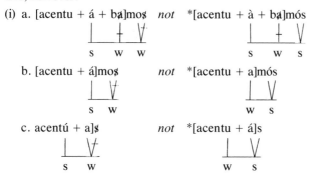

(i) a. [acentu + á + ba]moş   *not*   *[acentu + à + ba]mós

          s w w   s w s

   b. [acentu + á]moş   *not*   *[acentu + a]mós

           s w   w s

   c. acentú + a]ş   *not*   *[acentu + á]s

           s w   w s

13. Arguments supporting this morphological analysis are given in Harris (1980b). Essentially the same constituency is proposed in Hooper and Terrell (1976), though the context and arguments are different.

14. Some vowel-final oxytones (e.g., *dominó*) are derivationally isolated, so that we cannot see how they behave in various morphological environments. Fortunately, however, this is not true in a broad and representative range of cases. Compare, for example, *papá/papacito* versus *papa/papita*, *café/cafetero* versus *molino/molinero* (*molinoero*), *Perú/peruano* versus *tribu/tribal* (*tribual*), and many more. The fact that terminal elements never appear inside derivational stems provides direct evidence that the indicated vowels of *papacito, cafetero, peruano,* etc., are not terminal elements.

15. A few words like *cowboy, jersey* can have either final or penultimate stress. In the latter case their status as anglicisms is obvious. *Jersey* has been nativized in some dialects as [xerséi], with obligatory final stress.

16. The parentheses in *s* (*w*) have their usual interpretation: *s* can be assigned

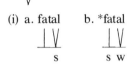

iff *s w* cannot, as in (ia) but not (ib), which violates the Branching Condition.

(i) a. fatal   b. *fatal

The parentheses in the labeling of word trees (immediately below in the text) are interpreted in the same way.

17. Harris (1980b) contains a general discussion of plural formation in Spanish, including the case of singulars and plurals that are not distinct, e.g., *tórax, hipótesis, tocadiscos,* etc.

18. These conditions cannot be stated in phonological terms: recall from part I that the rhyme Vns of *jovens* is phonologically well formed in Spanish, as are all VCs rhymes.

19. This example apparently provides some support for the argument against "deforestation" given in Kiparsky (1979). Suppose that the tree structure erected in the first cycle of *jóven* were erased and then rebuilt in the second cycle on the representation *joven + es*. After stem-final *-n* becomes an onset, no record of its extrametricality remains in the rhyme projection. Normal foot construction would then give (i).

(i) *jovén + es

Of course, a convention could be invented according to which the extrametricality of the resyllabified consonant would be transferred onto its ex-rhyme-mate, thus guaranteeing (ii).

(ii) jóven + es

But no such convention is needed if there is no deforestation.

20. Strong Foot-Label Erasure will be easily recognized in this example as the prosodic reincarnation of the rule "Erase all nonrightmost stresses in a word," which has been discussed in Harris (1969 (for example, section 4.3.4)) and other works.

21. The ensuing discussion involves a rule of syllable structure. There are also purely segmental rules (e.g., rules that change the point of articulation of consonants) that are sensitive to prosodic structure and whose effects persist after alteration of this structure destroys their environment. Discussion is found in section 3.1 and following sections.

22. Sequences of the form #(C)rGV́... are not automatically ruled out on purely segmental phonological grounds; cf. well-formed *griéta, pruéba, priéto, ruído*, etc. Incidentally, *riíto* 'river' (dim.) is unmistakably distinct from *rito* 'rite'.

23. This example apparently provides another piece of evidence against "deforestation" (cf. note 19). If deforestation occurred at the outset of the second cycle, we would have not *gru + ita, ri + ito* but *gru + ita, ri + ito*. It is hard to see a principled reason (though easy to invent a condition ad hoc) why Desyllabification should not apply to produce **gru + ita, *ri + ito*, just as it does in *peru + ano → peru + ano*, etc.

Appendix

1. And we should certainly not base theoretical proposals on them, as I did in Harris (1973, section 3).

2. This is similar to a proposal by Hooper and Terrell (1976). They analyze *régimen* as *régim + en* and assert that *-en* is a terminal element, which in their terms places *-en* outside the domain of stress. There are problems with these claims. First, the correct analysis into morphemes must be *reg + i + men* (cf. *reg + i + r, reg + e + nte* on the one hand, and *cert + a + men, abdo + men, volu + men* on the other). Second, *-en* does not behave morphologically like a terminal element. Undisputed terminal elements occur only at the outer layer of morphological structure—they cannot be followed by derivational affixes. But *-en*, or more accurately *-men*, can be followed by derivational affixes (in which case it has the shape *-min*), for example, *certamin + ar, abdomin + al, volumin + oso*, etc.

3. So far as I know, the only remaining words that have antepenultimate stress in a consonant-final derivational stem are *asíndeton* and *bustrófedon*. It is nearly impossible to find anyone who has heard of either word in the singular, much less the plural. The plural of *Júpiter,* if it has one, was mentioned in note 6 of chapter 5.

References

Alba, O. (1979). "Análisis fonológico de /r/ y /l/ implosivas en un dialecto rural dominicano," *Boletín de la Academia Puertorriqueña de la Lengua Española* 7, 1–18.

Bell, A., and J. Hooper, eds. (1978). *Syllables and Segments*, North-Holland, Amsterdam.

Brame, M. K. (1974). "The Cycle in Phonology: Stress in Palestinian, Maltese, and Spanish," *Linguistic Inquiry* 5, 39–60.

Canfield, D. L. (1962). *La pronunciación del español en América*, Publicaciones del Instituto Caro y Cuervo XVII, Bogotá.

Chomsky, N. (1970). "Remarks on Nominalization," in R. A. Jacobs and P. S. Rosenbaum, eds., *Readings in English Transformational Grammar*, Ginn, Waltham, Massachusetts, 184–221.

Chomsky, N. (1980). *Rules and Representations*, Columbia University Press, New York.

Chomsky, N. (1981). *Lectures on Government and Binding*, Foris, Dordrecht.

Chomsky, N., and M. Halle (1968). *The Sound Pattern of English*, Harper & Row, New York.

Chomsky, N., M. Halle, and F. Lukoff (1956). "On Accent and Juncture in English," *For Roman Jakobson*, Mouton, The Hague.

Clements, G. N., and K. Ford (1979). "Kikuyu Tone Shift and Its Synchronic Consequences," *Linguistic Inquiry* 10, 179–210.

Contreras, H. (1968). "Vowel Fusion in Spanish," *Hispania* 52, 60–62.

Contreras, H. (1977). "Spanish Epenthesis and Stress," *Working Papers in Linguistics* 3, University of Washington, Seattle, Washington, 9–33.

Contreras, H., and S. Saporta (1960). "The Validation of a Phonological Grammar," *Lingua* 9, 1–15.

Foley, J. A. (1965). *Spanish Morphology*, Doctoral dissertation, MIT, Cambridge, Massachusetts.

Fudge, E. (1969). "Syllables," *Journal of Linguistics* 5, 253–286.

García-Bellido, P. (1979). "Trilled vs. Flapped /r/: Some Remarks on the Syllable Structure of Spanish," presented at NELS X, University of Ottawa, Ottawa, Ontario.

Goldsmith, J. (1976a). *Autosegmental Phonology*, Doctoral dissertation, MIT, Cambridge, Massachusetts. Available from the Indiana University Linguistics Club, Bloomington, Indiana.

Goldsmith, J. (1976b). "An Overview of Autosegmental Phonology," *Linguistic Analysis* 2, 23–68.

Golibart, P. (1976). *Cibaeño Vocalization*, Master's thesis, University of Kansas, Lawrence, Kansas.

Guitart, J. M. (1979). "On the True Environment for Weakening and Deletion in Consonant-Weak Spanish Dialects," presented at the Conference on Non-English Language Variation in the Western Hemisphere, University of Louisville, Kentucky.

Guitart, J. M. (1980a). "En torno a la sílaba como entidad fonemática en los dialectos del Caribe hispánico," presented at the V Simposio de Dialectología del Caribe Hispánico, Caracas, Venezuela.

Guitart, J. M. (1980b). "Some Theoretical Implications of Liquid Gliding in Cibaeño Dominican Spanish," presented at the X Linguistic Symposium on Romance Languages, University of Washington, Seattle, Washington. [Published in 1981 in H. Contreras and J. Klausenburger, eds., *Proceedings of the Tenth Anniversary Symposium on Romance Linguistics,* supplement II to *Papers in Linguistics* 3, University of Washington, Seattle, Washington, 223–228.]

Halle, M. (1980). "Formal vs. Functional Considerations in Phonology," in B. Brogyanyi, ed., *Studies in Diachronic, Synchronic, and Typological Linguistics,* John Benjamins, Amsterdam, 325–341.

Halle, M., and J.-R. Vergnaud (1980). "Three Dimensional Phonology," *Journal of Linguistic Research* 1, 83–105.

Halle, M., and J.-R. Vergnaud (in preparation). *Three Dimensional Phonology.*

Harris, J. W. (1969). *Spanish Phonology,* MIT Press, Cambridge, Massachusetts.

Harris, J. W. (1972). "Five Classes of Irregular Verbs in Spanish," in J. Casagrande and B. Saciuk, eds., *Generative Studies in Romance Languages,* Newbury House, Rowley, Massachusetts, 247–271.

Harris, J. W. (1973). "On the Order of Certain Phonological Rules in Spanish," in S. R. Anderson and P. Kiparsky, eds., *A Festschrift for Morris Halle,* Holt, Rinehart and Winston, New York, 59–76.

Harris, J. W. (1974). "Morphologization of Phonological Rules: An Example from Chicano Spanish," in R. J. Campbell, M. G. Goldin, and M. C. Wang, eds., *Linguistic Studies in Romance Languages,* Georgetown University Press, Washington, D.C., 8–27.

Harris, J. W. (1975). "Stress Assignment Rules in Spanish," in W. G. Milán, J. J. Staczek, and J. C. Zamora, eds., *1974 Colloquium on Spanish and Portuguese Linguistics,* Georgetown University Press, Washington, D.C.

Harris, J. W. (1977a). "Aspects of Spanish Verb Morphology," in M. P. Hagiwara, ed., *Studies in Romance Linguistics,* Newbury House, Rowley, Massachusetts, 44–60.

Harris, J. W. (1977b). "Remarks on Diphthongization in Spanish," *Lingua* 41, 261–305.

Harris, J. W. (1977c). "Spanish Vowel Alternations, Diacritic Features, and the Structure of the Lexicon," in J. A. Kegl, D. Nash, and A. Zaenen, eds., *Proceedings of the Seventh Annual Meeting of the North Eastern Linguistic Society,* MIT, Cambridge, Massachusetts.

Harris, J. W. (1980a). "Lo morfológico en una gramática generativa: alternancias vocálicas en las formas verbales del español," in J. M. Guitart and J. Roy, eds., *La estructura fónica de la lengua castellana y la lingüística generativo-transformacional,* Anagrama, Barcelona, 141–199.

Harris, J. W. (1980b). "Nonconcatenative Morphology and Spanish Plurals," *Journal of Linguistic Research* 1, 15–31.

Harris, J. W. (1980c). "Palatal-φ Alternations in Spanish," in F. H. Nuessel, Jr., ed., *Contemporary Studies in Romance Languages,* Indiana University Linguistics Club, Bloomington, Indiana, 108–130.

Harris, J. W. (ms.). "Explorations in Spanish Word-Structure: An X-Bar Theory," unpublished manuscript.

Harris, J. W. (forthcoming). "Autosegmental Phonology, Lexical Phonology, and Nasal Consonants in Spanish" (preliminary version presented at Symposium on Phonological Representations, Cornell University, July 24, 1981).

Hayes, B. P. (1979). "Extrametricality," in K. Safir, ed., *Papers on Syllable Structure, Metrical Structure and Harmony Processes,* MIT Working Papers in Linguistics 1, 77–87.

Hayes, B. P. (1980). *A Metrical Theory of Stress Rules,* Doctoral dissertation, MIT, Cambridge, Massachusetts.

Hooper, J. B. (1972). "The Syllable in Phonological Theory," *Language* 48, 525–540.

Hooper, J. B. (1976). *An Introduction to Natural Generative Phonology,* Academic Press, New York.

Hooper, J. B., and T. Terrell (1976). "Stress Assignment in Spanish: A Natural Generative Analysis," *Glossa* 10, 64–110.

Hutchinson, S. P. (1974). "Spanish Vowel Sandhi," *Papers from the Parasession on Natural Phonology,* Chicago Linguistic Society, Chicago, Illinois, 184–191.

Jaeggli, O. (1980). "Spanish Diminutives," in F. H. Nuessel, Jr., ed., *Contemporary Studies in Romance Languages,* Indiana University Linguistics Club, Bloomington, Indiana, 142–158.

Kahn, D. (1976). *Syllable-Based Generalizations in English Phonology,* Doctoral dissertation, MIT, Cambridge, Massachusetts. Available from the Indiana University Linguistics Club, Bloomington, Indiana.

Kaye, J., and J. Lowenstamm (1979). "Syllable Structure and Markedness Theory," presented at the IV GLOW Conference, Pisa, Italy.

Kiparsky, P. (1979). "Metrical Structure Assignment Is Cyclic," *Linguistic Inquiry* 10, 421–441.

Liberman, M. Y. (1975). *The Intonational System of English,* Doctoral dissertation, MIT, Cambridge, Massachusetts.

Liberman, M. Y., and A. Prince (1977). "On Stress and Linguistic Rhythm," *Linguistic Inquiry* 8, 249–336.

Lozano, M. (1979). *Stop and Spirant Alternations: Fortition and Spirantization Processes in Spanish Phonology,* Doctoral dissertation, Indiana University, Bloomington, Indiana. Available from the Indiana University Linguistics Club, Bloomington, Indiana.

McCarthy, J. J. (1979a). *Formal Problems in Semitic Phonology and Morphology,* Doctoral dissertation, MIT, Cambridge, Massachusetts.

McCarthy, J. J. (1979b). "On Stress and Syllabification," *Linguistic Inquiry* 10, 443–466.

Mascaró, J. (1976). *Catalan Phonology and the Phonological Cycle,* Doctoral dissertation, MIT, Cambridge, Massachusetts. Available from the Indiana University Linguistics Club, Bloomington, Indiana.

Mohanan, K. P. (1981). "Lexical Phonology and Compounding in Malayalam," presented at the Trilateral Workshop on Nonlinear Phonology, University of Texas, Austin, April 10–12.

Mohanan, K. P. (1982). *Lexical Phonology,* Doctoral dissertation, MIT, Cambridge, Massachusetts.

Navarro Tomás, T. (1965). *Manual de pronunciación española,* Consejo Superior de Investigaciones Científicas, Madrid.

Pesetsky, D. (1979). "Russian Morphology and Lexical Theory," unpublished paper, MIT, Cambridge, Massachusetts.

Pike, K., and E. Pike (1947). "Immediate Constituents of Mazateco Syllables," *International Journal of American Linguistics* 13, 78–91.

Real Academia Española (1973). *Esbozo de una nueva gramática de la lengua española*, Espasa-Calpe, Madrid.

Rotenberg, J. (1978). *The Syntax of Phonology*, Doctoral dissertation, MIT, Cambridge, Massachusetts.

Rubach, J. (1980). "Segmental Rules of English and Cyclic Phonology," unpublished paper, Instytut Anglistyki, University of Warsaw.

Rubach, J. (forthcoming). *Cyclic Phonology and Palatalization in Polish and English*, Warsaw University Press, Warsaw.

Safir, K., ed. (1979). *Papers on Syllable Structure, Metrical Structure and Harmony Processes*, MIT Working Papers in Linguistics 1.

Saporta, S., and H. Contreras (1962). *A Phonological Grammar of Spanish*, University of Washington Press, Seattle, Washington.

Selkirk, E. (1972). *The Phrase Phonology of English and French*, Doctoral dissertation, MIT, Cambridge, Massachusetts.

Selkirk, E. (1974). "French Liaison and the $\overline{\text{X}}$ Notation," *Linguistic Inquiry* 5, 573–590.

Selkirk, E. (1978). "On Prosodic Structure and Its Relation to Syntactic Structure," presented at the Conference on Mental Representation in Phonology, sponsored by the Sloan Foundation.

Selkirk, E. (1980). "The Role of Prosodic Categories in English Word Stress," *Linguistic Inquiry* 11, 563–605.

Selkirk, E. (in preparation). *Phonology and Syntax: The Relationship between Sound and Structure*.

Solan, L. (1979). "Spanish Stress," in J. Lowenstamm, ed., *University of Massachusetts Working Papers in Linguistics* 4, Amherst, Massachusetts.

Stockwell, R. P., J. D. Bowen, and I. Silva-Fuenzalida (1956). "Spanish Juncture and Intonation," *Language* 32, 641–665.

Suñer, M. (1975). "Spanish Adverbs: Support for the Phonological Cycle?" *Linguistic Inquiry* 6, 602–605.

Terrell, T. D. (1975). "Functional Constraints on the Deletion of Word-Final /s/ in Cuban Spanish," in *Proceedings of the First Annual Meeting of the Berkeley Linguistics Society*, Berkeley Linguistics Society, Berkeley, California, 431–437.

Terrell, T. D. (1978a). "La aspiración y elisión en el español porteño," *Anuario de Letras* (Universidad Nacional Autónoma de México) 16, 41–66.

Terrell, T. D. (1978b). "Sobre la aspiración y elisión de /s/ en el español de Puerto Rico," *Nueva Revista de Filología Hispánica* 27, 24–38.

Terrell, T. D. (1979). "Final -s in Cuban Spanish," *Hispania* 62, 599–612.

Vergnaud, J.-R. (1979). "Formal Phonology," in J. Lowenstamm, ed., *University of Massachusetts Occasional Papers* 10.

Whitley, S. (1976). "Stress in Spanish: Two Approaches," *Lingua* 39, 301–332.